QUIT & STAY QUIT

A Personal Program to Stop Smoking

TERRY A. RUSTIN, M.D.

HAZELDEN

Hazelden
Center City, Minnesota

©1991, 1994 by Terry A. Rustin, M.D.
All rights reserved. Published 1991. Second Edition 1994
Printed in the United States of America. No portion of
this publication may be reproduced in any manner
without the written permission of the publisher

10 09 08 07   13 12 11

Library of Congress Cataloging-in-Publication Data
Rustin, Terry A.
    Quit and stay quit : a personal program to stop smoking / Terry A.
Rustin.
      p.   cm.
    "A slightly revised ed. of the same title."
    Includes bibliographical references and index.
    ISBN 13: 978-1-56838-109-1
    1. Cigarette smokers—Rehabilitation.   2. Tobacco habit—Treatment.
3. Self-help techniques.   I. Title.
    HV5740.R77   1996
    613'.85—dc20   95-52695
                                                          CIP

QUIT & STAY QUIT

This book is dedicated to the memory of Ted R., one of the finest addiction counselors I ever knew. Ted's recovery from alcoholism was an inspiration to many; his professional work in recovery treatment helped hundreds of alcoholics and drug addicts reshape their lives. Ted never took a drink as long as I knew him, but he was rarely without a cigarette. He would probably still be working with addicts today had he not died from cancer. Ted was one of 300,000 Americans who died prematurely that year because of tobacco. I dedicate this book to his memory, that others may recover.

Contents

Acknowledgments

For their help and support in the creation of this book I want to thank the many colleagues and patients who have helped me understand what dependence on nicotine and smoking is like, and the many others who have encouraged me to provide some tangible material to help smokers recover from their addiction. I owe particular thanks to the physicians, staff, and administration of the Student Health Service at the University of Houston, where I ran my first successful smoking cessation groups; and to my wife, Laura, who has patiently reviewed every version of this material since 1985.

I am especially grateful to my editor, Tim McIndoo, who believed in the importance and potential of this project when others did not. If you find this book of value in your own recovery, Tim's patient editing deserves much of the credit.

– PART I –

Get Ready . . .

Getting Started: Goals of Part I

Welcome to an opportunity.

Most smokers have a part that wants to quit and a part that wants to keep smoking. This book recognizes both parts of you. Today, the part that wants to keep on smoking may be bigger and stronger than the part that wants to become smoke-free. That's normal.

You know you will be better off when you quit smoking, but you have not yet succeeded in quitting. You may have tried to quit several times in the past and suffered so much you gave up the effort. With the help of this book, you can succeed and become smoke-free without undue suffering as long as you are willing to keep reading and working the projects in the pages ahead.

You may have tried other methods to quit smoking. Perhaps you once tossed away your cigarettes, vowing never to smoke again. Perhaps you took acupuncture treatments, hypnosis, injections in the nose, or aversion therapy that made you puff until you felt nauseated. One of your friends may have recommended you try a new method. If there is a method that appeals to you, by all means give it a try. Your goal should be to quit smoking, and you should select a system you believe will work for you.

But if you're still looking for help, *Quit and Stay Quit* may be just right for you. In this book you will learn about tobacco and you will also learn a great deal about yourself. You will identify your own goals and will work toward them at your own pace. You can do this by yourself, with someone you trust, in a small group, with a self-help group, or with a therapist. This book is about making it possible to reach your own goals. Do you know what your goals are?

Some people know exactly what they want to achieve in life. They prefer dealing with details, facts, and things they can see, touch, and measure. Accordingly, their goals are very specific. Others have a general sense about where they are headed. They prefer to deal with concepts; thus their goals are general ones.

What are your goals for smoking? If you're a detail-oriented person, perhaps you have made a plan to cut down or to quit. You might even have a timetable already. Many detail-oriented people, however, make the same quit-smoking plan year after year but never put it into action, and then become angry at themselves when their plans fail. If this sounds like your pattern, this book will help you reach your goals by showing you some of the "big picture" about smoking.

If you're an imaginative person who is not good with details, you might envision yourself quitting someday, but you're not sure when. You may have talked about your plan with friends and family but have been unable to put your hopes into action. You may have felt inadequate or unworthy because you could not succeed in the way others have. If this sounds like your pattern, this book will help you reach your goals by showing you step by step how to quit smoking.

We call this book *Quit and Stay Quit* because *staying quit* is more important than quitting. People quit smoking all the time, only to start again. But success means staying quit. In this program, we don't care if you quit today, or tomorrow, or next week, or next month. You will determine your own Quit Day. The most important thing is that when you quit, you *stay* quit. If you stick with this program, the chances are good that you will succeed.

Most smokers have made attempts at quitting before. Research shows that most successful quitters made at least three serious attempts before succeeding. In the past, you may have thought of a "quitter" as a loser and a failure, but when it comes to smoking, a "quitter" is a winner and a success. You, too, can be one of those winners.

However, be aware that powerful forces are trying to keep you stuck right where you are, trying to keep you from achieving your goals, trying to get you to start smoking again each time you quit for a while. One of these forces is the nicotine in your cigarettes. Another is the relentless advertising and promotions by the tobacco companies. Another is the belief that everyone except you is at risk for emphysema or lung cancer—every smoker is in denial to some degree. Another is the fact that insurance companies will pay a doctor to treat your lung cancer but are reluctant to pay anyone to treat your dependence on smoking.

Another problem is the confusion in our government about tobacco. One government office spends millions of dollars supporting tobacco farming with subsidies. Another one spends millions of dollars researching better treatments for lung and heart ailments caused by smoking. Another part promotes cigarette sales around the world. Another part tells us about the dangers of smoking and encourages us to quit.

But doctors and scientists are not confused. They know that tobacco is a deadly product. They know it's not a food—no one uses it for its nutritional value. They know it's not a drug—it doesn't cure or prevent disease. In fact, it causes disease.

Most smokers would like to quit but are concerned they will gain weight, become extremely irritable, or worse. Many smokers are afraid they cannot do without cigarettes. Some are afraid of trying to quit and failing. Some smokers have quit for a while but became so depressed, confused, or inefficient that they started smoking again. If you feel this way, you have had lots of company over the last 350 years.

The native peoples of the Western Hemisphere (American Indians, Mayans, Aztecs, and others) invented tobacco smoking. They used it for traditional ceremonies and for relaxation. Sir Walter Raleigh brought tobacco back to England in the sixteenth century. At the time, social critics thought it was a disgusting, degenerate habit. But people took it up anyway and paid plenty for the pleasure, since the tobacco had to be brought from halfway around the world. Tobacco became an important crop in the Southern states in pre-Revolutionary America.

Times haven't changed all that much.

About 26 percent of American men and about 24 percent of American women still smoke. These numbers decrease a little bit every year. Until recently, fewer teenage girls than boys smoked, but the girls have caught up, and today about 18 percent of all teenagers smoke. Smokeless tobacco has recently become more popular among teenage boys, and in some states, up to 6 percent of these boys use smokeless tobacco daily.

But the percentage of American *physicians* who smoke has dropped steadily, year by year. Of California physicians, about 50 percent were smokers in 1950, compared with 10 percent in 1980. In 1995, only 3 percent of American physicians smoked.

In 1950, nobody suspected that smoking was much of a problem. Everyone smoked, it seemed, and research on the relationship between smoking and illness was just beginning. Then in 1964, the surgeon general of the United States told us that cigarette smoking could be a danger to our health, and all of a sudden people began to wonder if they should quit.

Doctors began paying attention to illnesses associated statistically with smoking. Researchers concluded that cigarette smoking was responsible for most cases of lung cancer, emphysema, and chronic bronchitis, and that it contributed to arteriosclerosis, heart attacks, high blood pressure, strokes, and many cancers. In fact, medical researchers found that cigarette smoking caused damage to every system they studied. Recent evidence shows that just living in the same house as a smoker can cause lung and heart damage to nonsmokers, especially children.

Industrial psychologists began looking at what happens when people smoke on the job. They discovered that workers who smoke are less efficient and waste the equivalent of a week or more each year by smoking. Airlines and restaurants opened nonsmoking sections, and insurance companies offered discounts to nonsmokers.

Health economists discovered that smoking costs the United States as much as $57 billion a year. Smoking causes health problems that result in lost work time, higher medical expenses, and greater fire hazards. The health cost of a pack of cigarettes is now more than two dollars. This means that for every pack of cigarettes you smoke, you will end up paying at least two dollars in increased health care costs during your lifetime.

Each year since 1964, the number of people giving up smoking has increased, and the number of people starting to smoke has decreased in every group except teenage girls (who are taking up smoking at a record rate). Today, only 18 percent of college graduates smoke, compared with 35 percent of high school dropouts.

Most smokers today believe they should quit. Every smoker knows several "helpful" people who don't hesitate to give free advice. Some of these folks go beyond friendly suggestions and become downright hostile about it. (Interestingly, many of these aggressive nonsmokers were themselves smokers. What sort of a former smoker will you be?)

You have picked up this book, *Quit and Stay Quit*, because you smoke and you would like to quit. Most smokers feel as you do. Surveys show that at least 85 percent of smokers would like to quit. So the question is, Why haven't they? Why haven't you?

Here are some of the reasons smokers keep smoking. Are some of them your reasons?

- I really enjoy smoking.
- Having a cigarette in my hand gives me something to do when I'm thinking.
- I like how I look with a cigarette—like the people I see in the cigarette ads.
- Nobody is going to tell me I have to quit smoking.
- I know me—I'll go nuts after about two hours.
- Everybody I know smokes, and I don't want to be different.
- I'd like to quit, but I don't think I can.
- I've quit before and started smoking again. I couldn't stand failing again.
- I'm afraid I'll gain weight.
- I don't get drunk, gamble, or mess around—a person has to have a little fun, right?

✎ *In a journal,* (page 21) *add a reason yourself—one of the reasons you want to keep smoking.*

All these reasons are good ones. Smoking does great things for many people. The nicotine helps them concentrate better and stay alert. The cigarette gives them something to do with their hands and mouths. For most smokers, smoking is a lot of fun. If there were no consequences to smoking, there would be no reason to quit.

Unfortunately, there are many consequences to smoking.

In this program, you will not see pictures of blackened lungs and bloody cancers, although tobacco can indeed damage your lungs and cause cancer. But you already knew that. If that knowledge had been enough to get you to quit, you would have quit already.

So we need to look at how smoking has interfered with your life. We need to search out your specific reasons for quitting smoking.

✎ *Take a moment to write down one of your reasons you want to quit smoking.*

✎ A good reason for me to quit smoking is . . .

Remember, your first reason does not have to be a perfect one. It's not so important *where* you start, but *that* you start. Can you think of another good reason for you to quit smoking?

✎ Another good reason for me to quit smoking is . . .

That's fine! How about one more?

✎ Another good reason for me to quit smoking is . . .

Excellent. You have just found three good reasons for you (not someone else) to quit smoking.

You may find that three reasons came easily to you. That may be because most of the reasons you have for wanting to quit smoking are not your reasons at all. Most of them are *somebody else's reasons.* Well, you might *quit* for somebody else's reasons, but you will only *stay* quit for your own reasons. When you were a teenager, *all* the reasons to quit were somebody else's reasons, and most still are: your parents' reasons, your spouse's reasons, your doctor's reasons, your boss's reasons . . . everybody's reasons except yours.

Some of your reasons will be *logical* reasons. Some of these reasons appear important at first but turn out to be much less so when looked at closely. The $800 you spend on cigarettes each year is an example of a logical reason—you wouldn't turn down a gift of $800, but $800 a year isn't enough to change your lifestyle significantly. If someone offered you $800 to quit smoking for a year, would you accept the offer? Probably not.

There are other logical reasons that seem important and *are* important; however, you haven't quit smoking because of them. Quitting smoking to avoid lung disease is an example. Everyone would agree this is a good reason to quit. It's sensible, significant, and important. But you've known for some time that cigarettes cause lung damage and you haven't quit yet. Many people who already have serious lung damage continue to smoke, so this logic hasn't helped them either.

Other people's reasons to quit smoking, as well as purely logical reasons to quit smoking—even when they are great reasons—will always be inadequate to get you to quit and stay quit. These reasons are good starting points, but you need to keep on looking.

With a little effort, you will discover your *personal* reasons. These reasons reflect how you see yourself as a person, your most sincere feelings, your real self. *These* are your most important reasons. *These* are the ones that are really your reasons. *These* are the ones for which you will quit and *stay* quit.

That's why we're going to search for your personal reasons.

Look back for a moment at the three reasons you wrote down a minute ago. Are they somebody else's reasons that you've accepted as your own? Are they logical reasons that make perfect sense but have been ineffective in getting you to change? Or are they personal reasons, reasons that really mean something to you?

See if you can make your three reasons more specific and more personal. Write down your new, expanded reasons near each original reason.

Here are some of the reasons other smokers have given for wanting to quit. Perhaps some of them are similar to your own:

1. A good reason for me to quit smoking is for my health.

That seems like a logical reason. (No one is going to deny that your health will improve if you quit smoking.) It could also be somebody else's reason for you to quit—your doctor's reason or your spouse's reason. How could you make it more personal?

1. A good reason for me to quit smoking is for my health—

    so I won't get emphysema like Uncle Charlie did.
    - I get scared just thinking about how he suffered; it was like he was suffocating all the time.
    - It was really unfair to Aunt Stella for him to keep smoking even after he was so sick.
    - I don't want my nephew to lose me the way I lost Uncle Charlie. I couldn't understand it when I was little, and I really felt abandoned.

    so I won't wake up with a cough each morning.
    - I cough up putrid green and yellow mucus.
    - My chest hurts and I have trouble catching my breath.
    - My wife shakes her head in a really patronizing way each time I cough and it ticks me off, but I can't really say anything about it because I know she's right.

    so I won't have to worry about getting cancer.
    - If I die now, who would support my family?
    - I want to see my kids grow up.
    - Hey—I'm smarter than that!

Can you see how these reasons became more personal as they were expanded? They became reasons worth quitting for.

Here's another example:

2. A good reason for me to quit smoking is so my clothes will smell better.

That looks like a logical reason. Your clothes *will* smell better after you have quit smoking. But that's not front-page news. This is really "somebody else's" reason—whoever has to smell the clothes in your closet. Smokers rarely notice the smell of stale cigarette smoke on their clothing because the smoke damages the nerve cells in the nose. As long as this reason remains somebody else's reason, it won't help you quit.

Can you expand it?

2. A good reason for me to quit smoking is so my clothes will smell better.
    - I won't have to send my outfits to the dry cleaner so often.
    - I won't be embarrassed when my mother comes to visit and peeks in my closet.
    - I'll be more confident when I meet someone for the first time.

What began as a logical reason became much more personal with just a little effort.

   3. A good reason for me to quit smoking is so my wife will be proud of me.

This is a good, solid, personal reason. But even this reason can become more personal:

   3. A good reason for me to quit smoking is so my wife will be proud of me.
- She'll know I can achieve a goal that's a real challenge.
- She'll trust me more when I make a promise.
- She'll look up to me more.
- How people see me is extremely important to me—I wonder what they think of me as a smoker?
- *I'll* be more proud of myself too.

This reason was already personal and became even better. Now here are some more reasons. Which ones apply to you?

   4. A good reason for me to quit smoking is that I spend about $800 a year on cigarettes, and I could use the money for something else.

What else? Why are you choosing cigarettes instead? What would it mean to you to take better care of yourself?

   5. A good reason for me to quit smoking is so I won't burn holes in the upholstery anymore.

Whose sofa did you burn a hole in? What was that experience like? How did it make you feel?

   6. A good reason for me to quit smoking is out of consideration for other people, such as those with respiratory problems.

What happened? Did you offend or unintentionally injure someone?

   7. A good reason for me to quit smoking is so I can sit in any part of a restaurant, smoking or nonsmoking.

Have you had a problem before? Are you angry at how smokers are restricted? Do you resent being told what to do?

8. A good reason for me to quit smoking is so I will like myself more.

Why?

Keep at it, because the more personal reasons you can develop, the more likely you will be to stay quit.

You can see that if you put your mind to it, you could eventually have *hundreds* of reasons for quitting smoking—most of which you were not aware of or only vaguely aware of. In your notebook, write down some of the reasons you have recently discovered.

But please do not stop there. Most of your reasons will have a negative tone to them. They will deal with failures, dying, losses, and embarrassment. We all dwell too much on the negatives in life as it is.

✎ *So go back to the reasons you have written down, and rewrite them into a positive format, like this:*

1. A good reason for me to quit smoking is for my health.
   When I'm a nonsmoker, I'll be really healthy.

2. A good reason for me to quit smoking is so I won't get emphysema like Uncle Charlie did.
   When I'm a nonsmoker, I'll breathe easily and deeply.

3. A good reason for me to quit smoking is so I won't cough up green mucus in the morning.
   When I'm a nonsmoker, I'll wake up with a sense of accomplishment and a feeling of freshness.

4. A good reason for me to quit smoking is so my wife will be proud of me.
   When I'm a nonsmoker, I'll have more self-respect.

5. A good reason for me to quit smoking is so I won't burn holes in the upholstery anymore.
   When I'm a nonsmoker, I won't embarrass myself or my friends by having to pay for upholstery repair.

For each of your reasons to quit smoking, compose a positive statement of hope and health and write it alongside or under the original reason. That way, every time you refer to your list for inspiration and confidence, you will remember not only the pain of your past, but also your optimism for the future.

By turning the pain into hope, you are beginning to see yourself as you would like to be. By saying, "When I'm a nonsmoker, I'll be able to breathe easily and deeply and I won't cough in the morning," you are visualizing the kind of person you are striving to become. You'll never get where you're headed if you don't recognize it when you get there. So knowing what you want from life and from yourself is a necessary step toward achieving your goals.

When you visualize yourself as a nonsmoker, you will be able to stay quit. Right now, you are a smoker who is not smoking (unless you're smoking while you're reading this). One day you will notice that you have begun to think of yourself as a nonsmoker, in the same way you think of yourself as a man or a woman. It will have become a part of you. When you achieve this, the craving for a cigarette will begin to fade, and it will feel as if a great weight has been lifted from your shoulders.

But this does not mean that you will be able to smoke again. Once you have become addicted to cigarettes, chances are you will always remain addicted to cigarettes. It's rare for anyone to be able to smoke "occasionally" after being a regular smoker, and it's probably not worth the risk.

Many people start off just wanting to cut down and later decide they are ready to quit. Some know they want to quit right from the start. Some "want to want to" quit. Wherever you are right now, you *can* become a nonsmoker—and if you stick with this program, you will.

Keep this book safe and your journal handy. One day when the weather is gloomy, you've had a fight with your husband or wife, you just got laid off, and you've discovered termites in your attic, the desire to smoke again may come over you very strongly. People relapse when they imagine that the advantages of smoking outweigh the disadvantages *at that moment.* If this happens to you, you can pull out this book and your journal and go over some of these reasons again. You will discover that you had some excellent reasons for wanting to quit—and that smoking a cigarette is not likely to solve the problems you are facing now.

This is a program of the future. You are not expected to toss away your cigarettes today or tomorrow or any time soon. Read through this book for a while first. You will be more successful at cutting down and quitting after you have established a foundation.

In the pages ahead, you will have the opportunity to look at the times you want a cigarette and why, and you will come up with alternatives to smoking in those situations. You will see what happened when you tried to quit before and discover what you need to do differently this time. You will read about the addictive nature of tobacco and how it has affected you. You will discover more about the role that tobacco plays in your life and what you can do about it. You will make specific plans that meet your goals.

Staying quit means that your attitude about smoking has changed. This takes time. If you try to quit prematurely, you will simply start smoking again; the relapse will increase your frustration, which in turn will make you want to smoke even more. So do not say "I've quit" until you are definitely ready.

This book will present information and examples and will offer questions for you to think about and answer in your journal. The details you add and the time you invest in this program will speed your progress toward quitting.

Invest, not spend. You are investing your time and effort in this program, and you can expect to reap rewards, as many have. You will not only learn about smoking and quitting, you will also learn a great deal about *yourself.* Through this program, you will discover a new freedom—freedom from tobacco.

Get ready . . .

2

Stages of Change I

Ed Koch, former mayor of New York City, was famous for stopping people on the street to ask, "How am I doing?" Knowing how you are doing will be helpful to you as you progress in your recovery from dependence on cigarettes.

While researching how people make the decision to quit smoking, psychologists Carlo DiClemente and James Prochaska developed the concept of "Stages of Change." This section will help you determine exactly where you are along this spectrum. There are similar sections in Parts II and III so that you can monitor your progress.

✎ *On the pages that follow, circle the* one *number on each ladder that best matches how you see yourself today.* **Circle only one number on each ladder.**

1. Contemplation Ladder

Please circle the *one* number on the ladder that most closely describes your thoughts and feelings about quitting smoking today.

10	I have decided to quit smoking.
9	
8	I am close to making a decision to quit smoking.
7	
6	I am thinking about quitting smoking, but I still have not made any
5	definite plans.
4	I am thinking about cutting down on my smoking, but I am not
3	thinking about quitting smoking.
2	I might have a problem with smoking, but I do not intend to cut
1	down or quit now.
0	I do not have a problem with smoking, and I do not intend to cut down or quit now.

2. Preparation Ladder

Please circle the *one* number on the ladder that most closely describes your thoughts and feelings about quitting smoking today.

10	I have decided to cut down on my smoking or to quit, and I have
9	already taken action.
8	I have decided to cut down on my smoking or to quit, and I expect
7	to take action within one week.
6	I have decided to cut down on my smoking or to quit, and I expect
5	to take action within one month.
4	I have decided to cut down on my smoking or to quit, and I expect
3	to take action within one year.
2	I have decided to cut down on my smoking or to quit—someday.
1	
0	I do not intend to cut down on my smoking or to quit.

3. Action Ladder

Please circle the *one* number on the ladder that most closely describes how actively you are working *today* on quitting smoking or preventing a relapse.

10 / **9**	I do something effective every day to cut down, quit, or prevent a relapse.
8 / **7**	I have done something effective today to cut down, quit, or prevent a relapse.
6 / **5**	I have done something effective within the last week to cut down, quit, or prevent a relapse.
4 / **3**	I have done something effective within the last month to cut down, quit, or prevent a relapse.
2 / **1**	I once took action to cut down, quit, or prevent a relapse, but I have not done so in more than one month.
0	I have *never* taken any action to cut down, quit, or prevent a relapse.

4. Abstinence Ladder

Please circle the *one* number on the ladder that most accurately describes how much you are smoking right now or how long it has been since your last cigarette.

10	I have not smoked in more than one year.
9 / **8**	I have not smoked in the last year.
7 / **6**	I have not smoked in the last thirty days.
5 / **4**	I have not smoked in the last seven days.
3 / **2**	I smoked less this week than I used to.
1 / **0**	I am smoking as much as or more than ever.

5. Maintenance Ladder

Please circle the *one* number on the ladder that most accurately describes the *longest* you have ever gone without smoking a cigarette since you became a regular smoker.

10	More than five years
9	
8	Two years
7	
6	Three months
5	
4	One week
3	
2	One day
1	
0	One hour

6. Relapse Ladder

Mark this ladder *only* if you did not smoke today.

Please circle the *one* number on the ladder that best describes how close you are to smoking again.

10	I no longer consider smoking again.
9	
8	I rarely consider smoking again.
7	
6	I occasionally consider smoking again.
5	
4	I frequently consider smoking again.
3	
2	I intend to smoke again.
1	
0	I have not yet started smoking again, but I have had a cigarette in my hand *within the last week* and almost smoked it.

Summary: Stages of Change Ladders

Record the number you circled on each ladder. The higher the numbers, the more progress you are making.

Date _____

    1. Contemplation _____
       (Thinking about quitting)

    2. Preparation _____
       (Making a decision to quit)

    3. Action _____
       (Taking action to quit)

    4. Abstinence _____
       (Staying quit now)

    5. Maintenance _____
       (My experience of staying quit)

    6. Relapse _____
       (Making sure I stay quit)

You will be able to measure your progress when you complete the similar sections in Parts II and III.

Cigarette Smoking Is an Addiction

An *addiction* is a disease. All chemical addictions are identified by the use of a mind- or mood-altering chemical and these three characteristics:

1. Tolerance
2. Withdrawal signs and symptoms
3. Addictive behaviors

A more complete portrait of addictive chemical use includes several other features:

4. The addict is preoccupied or obsessed with using the chemical.
5. The addict craves the chemical.
6. The addict rationalizes the chemical use.
7. The addict continues to use in spite of good reasons not to.
8. The chemical becomes more important than family, friends, job, ethics, or money.
9. The addict who starts using again after a period of abstinence quickly resumes his or her previous patterns and quantity of chemical use.
10. The addict sneaks and hides the chemical.
11. The addict chooses friends, jobs, and recreation that permit the continued use of the chemical, avoiding friends, jobs, and recreation that cannot accommodate the chemical use.
12. Physical deterioration begins, but the chemical use continues.

These concepts are not new. Back in 1952, Dr. E. M. Jellinek described most of them among his forty-three identifiable factors in the progression of alcoholism. And they may be familiar to you in reference to a heroin addict, a cocaine addict, or a marijuana smoker—but in reference to a cigarette smoker?

The potential to produce addiction is a characteristic of certain chemicals. Tobacco is a *compound* (a mixture of chemicals) that contains many addictive chemicals. Of these, the best studied is nicotine, which is found in all tobacco, smoked and smokeless.

Nicotine (named after Jean Nicot, the French ambassador to Portugal who introduced tobacco to the French royal court) stimulates the central nervous system. It resembles amphetamine and cocaine in many ways. In an important study by Dr. Jack Henningfield, subjects in a laboratory could not distinguish between injections of nicotine, cocaine, and amphetamine. All three have the same effects on the body: they raise the blood pressure, speed up the pulse, and cause the tiny blood vessels in the body to constrict. They also have the same effect on the mind: in low doses, they make subjects more alert, more attentive, and more adept at tasks that require complex thinking; but in high doses, they can cause confusion and severe anxiety.

Acetaldehyde is another of the mind- and mood-altering chemicals in cigarette smoke. When you drink alcohol, your liver breaks it down to acetaldehyde, which probably acts like a sedative on the brain and thus may be responsible for the calming effect a cigarette has on some people. Researchers believe that acetaldehyde can combine with other chemicals in your brain to produce chemicals (called tetrahydroisoquinolones, or TIQs) much like morphine, so it is conceivable that acetaldehyde plays a role in the addiction to tobacco. Very little research has been done on acetaldehyde because it is extremely difficult to measure.

Future research may demonstrate that several chemicals in tobacco smoke cause addiction. Today we know that nicotine does. When some researchers in England removed all the nicotine from cigarettes, they couldn't even give them away. Even though the experimental cigarettes tasted the same as cigarettes with nicotine, smokers could tell the difference, because the non-nicotine cigarettes did not give them the same feeling.

Perhaps you're not aware of how much of an effect your smoking has on your mind. Take a moment to ask yourself these questions:

- When I'm tired and lethargic, does a cigarette perk me up?
- When I'm anxious and tense, does a cigarette calm me down?
- When I have trouble concentrating, does a cigarette help me think better?

What an incredible product! It can perk you up when you are tired, calm you down when you are tense, and help you think more clearly. It improves your attention span, helps you make quick decisions and solve complex problems, and keeps you alert when you need to be.

If it were not for the consequences of tobacco use, there would be no earthly reason for you to quit.

People who use other addictive drugs, such as heroin, cocaine, and alcohol, are in a similar situation: they do not want to quit until they experience real consequences or until they recognize the inevitability of future consequences.

Is being hooked on smoking the same thing as being addicted to powerful drugs like heroin, cocaine, and alcohol? Addicts who use heroin and cocaine commit serious crimes for their drugs; smokers do not. Alcohol is involved in most traffic accidents and fatalities; tobacco is not. But remember, tobacco costs the nation some $57 billion a year in avoidable illnesses, fires, and lost productivity; and each pack of cigarettes you smoke will ultimately cost two dollars in health care expenses. Secretary of Health and Human Services Louis W. Sullivan, M.D., reported in 1990 that tobacco was responsible for 390,000 premature deaths in the United States each year. The 1995 estimate was for 430,000 premature deaths in the United States and 25,000 in Canada—more than three times as many as for all other addicting drugs *combined*.

Alcoholics get liver, heart, brain, and digestive diseases from their drinking, but they generally get a second, third, or fourth chance—they usually recover from their illnesses when they stop drinking. Smokers are rarely so fortunate. The diseases caused by tobacco (stroke, heart disease, lung and other cancers, and emphysema) tend to occur toward the end of life, and are usually fatal. The good news, as reported by

Surgeon General Antonia Novello in 1990, is that if smokers quit smoking before they get one of these serious complications, their health improves and they live much longer.

So if the consequences are severe, but people continue to smoke, there must be a reason: nicotine is addicting.

TOLERANCE

Tolerance means that over time, a chemical produces less and less of an effect; thus the user requires more of the chemical to be satisfied. There is a practical limit to the amount most users eventually take on a daily basis. For comparison, here is a table showing some addictive chemicals and the quantities users typically reach:

Chemical	How used	Amount used at plateau
alcohol	swallowed	1 quart of whiskey/day or 24 cans of beer/day
barbiturates	swallowed	40 capsules/day
heroin	injected	8 grams/day ($250)
crack cocaine	smoked	15 grams/day ($400)
Valium	swallowed	8 10-mg tablets/day
marijuana	smoked	5 joints/day
cigarettes	smoked	40 cigarettes/day

There are alcoholics who drink three quarts of whiskey a day, barbiturate addicts who take sixty capsules a day, Valium addicts who use two hundred milligrams a day, marijuana addicts who smoke twenty-five joints a day, and cigarette smokers who use eighty cigarettes a day. But drug use in these quantities is unusual; the table shows more common ones.

It might surprise you to see cigarettes (which cause limited social disruption) in the same table with crack cocaine and heroin (over which people have been murdered, societies have been torn apart, and nations have gone to war). However, more Americans are addicted to cigarettes than to any of the other chemicals. Although the social and physical effects of these chemicals vary, each of them has one thing in common with the others—it has addictive properties. *Tolerance* is one of the properties of addictive drugs.

When you smoked your very first cigarette, you probably got light-headed and a little giddy; perhaps your stomach growled and you got a bit queasy. Soon, you no longer felt that way after one or even two cigarettes, but if you smoked three in a row, you would. Today, you never feel like that, even after chain-smoking half a pack. This is tolerance. Tolerance is neither good nor bad; rather, it is a characteristic of some chemicals—addictive ones.

As time progressed, you smoked more cigarettes each day. At first, a pack lasted all week; soon, a pack lasted three days. You reached a milestone when you opened a new pack every day. Then it was a carton every week. You may be smoking two cartons a week by now. This is tolerance.

From the beginning, you noticed that you really wanted a cigarette at certain times. Eventually, you *needed* a cigarette at certain times. Initially, one puff was sufficient to calm you down. Later, it took several puffs. Once, a short puff held in your lungs just a fraction of a second was sufficient. Today you may need two or three deep drags held in your lungs for several seconds. This is tolerance.

Teenagers report that they *start* smoking to be part of the crowd, to be liked, and to act grown-up. The reason they most commonly give for *continuing* to smoke is that smoking gives them a "buzz"—a cheap, easily obtained, relatively legal buzz. After smoking for several years, however, most smokers rarely if ever notice the buzz. This, too, is tolerance.

✎ *What signs of tolerance have you noticed in yourself? In the exercise below and in similar exercises that follow, check all that apply to you and add one of your own.*

    ❏ I smoke more than I used to.
    ❏ I smoke more of each cigarette than I used to.

❑ I inhale very deeply.

❑ I get a buzz only from the very first cigarette in the morning.

❑ Smoking Carltons is like smoking nothing.

❑ After not smoking all day, my first cigarette gives me a buzz, but by the third cigarette, I no longer feel a buzz.

❑ I get up to smoke a cigarette in the middle of the night.

❑ I chain-smoke.

❑ I often smoke two cigarettes in a row.

❑ I used Nicorette gum and it did not make me light-headed.

❑ I used Nicorette gum and smoked too.

❑ I really do not think smoking affects my mind at all.

and _____

WITHDRAWAL

Withdrawal means that when you stop using a chemical, you develop signs and symptoms that are consistent, that are reproducible, and that can be relieved by the use of the chemical in question (or one very closely related to it). Signs are the things an observer can detect, such as rapid heartbeat, sweating, diarrhea, and seizures. Symptoms are things that you might complain of but cannot see, such as anxiety, craving, depression, or paranoid thoughts.

Two people withdrawing from the same drug or similar drugs will look very much the same; two people withdrawing from drugs from different drug groups will look very different. For example, two addicts withdrawing from Valium will show the same signs and symptoms. An addict withdrawing from Valium will show much the same symptoms as an addict withdrawing from alcohol, since Valium and alcohol are both sedatives. An addict withdrawing from heroin (an opioid drug) will show very different signs and symptoms than one withdrawing from Valium or alcohol.

Addicts soon discover that at some point after their last use of their chemical, withdrawal begins. They also learn that using their chemical again, or one similar to it, alleviates the pain of withdrawal. Each addictive chemical has a characteristic pattern of withdrawal.

The acute withdrawal from nicotine lasts about a week; less intense withdrawal may continue for several more weeks. You may have many of the possible signs and symptoms, or you may have only a few. Some people are overwhelmed by these symptoms, while others are bothered very little.

The common withdrawal symptoms you may have include irritability, light-headedness, mood swings, confusion, drowsiness, and insomnia. Some people have difficulty concentrating and remembering things. Dozens of research studies by Dr. Neil Benowitz, Dr. Judith Okene, Dr. Richard Hurt, and many others have shown that these symptoms develop when your body and brain do not get the amount of nicotine they are used to. When nicotine is given in amounts comparable to that in a cigarette, the symptoms go away.

You smoke some of your cigarettes to treat withdrawal symptoms; you also have many moments each day when you want to smoke, but only a few of them are caused by withdrawal. Withdrawal occurs when the level of nicotine in your bloodstream drops; this only happens when you have not had a cigarette in several hours.

Heroin addicts use heroin to stay out of withdrawal, but they rarely use *just enough* to stay out of withdrawal—they want to get high. Alcoholics take a drink to stay out of withdrawal, but they rarely drink *just enough* to stay out of withdrawal—they want to get drunk.

Similarly, you *do* use nicotine to stay out of withdrawal, but if you are like most smokers, one cigarette in the morning and two or three puffs each hour would be enough to keep you out of withdrawal. The strong desire you have to smoke at other times comes not from withdrawal, but from the desire for the chemical effect of a cigarette or the desire for the satisfaction of smoking a cigarette. Oftentimes you associate smoking with something in the world around you, as the following examples will illustrate:

You haven't had a cigarette in an hour, but you've been busy with other things and aren't thinking about smoking. You look up from your desk to see a friend lighting up a Winston—your brand. You are overcome with the desire for a cigarette.

This is not withdrawal. You associate *seeing* a cigarette with *smoking* one. Your symptoms are from the desire to obtain the cigarette effect— not to relieve withdrawal.

> *You return home to find a message from your doctor on your answering machine. "I don't want to frighten you unnecessarily," he says, "but the results of your blood tests were, well, uh, somewhat unexpected. Give me a call so we can talk about them." You reach for your Camels even before you turn off the machine.*

This isn't withdrawal either. It's your need to reduce the anxiety of that moment with a chemical you know will work—the chemical in your cigarette. You want it in your body as quickly as possible, so you smoke it as rapidly as possible.

> *You're having a fight with your husband, and you are getting nowhere. He sits down—plunk!—in front of the television and ignores you. Seething, you charge into another room, slam the door, and light a Virginia Slims. You stand there smoking it, about to boil over. You smoke another one and soon feel a little calmer.*

You felt the need for those cigarettes, but it wasn't because of withdrawal. You used the cigarette and its nicotine like medication to deal with your rage.

Withdrawal occurs only when the nicotine level drops. For most smokers, this happens just a few times each day. You break down half of the nicotine in your body about every two hours, so most smokers begin to feel withdrawal symptoms about three or four hours after their last cigarette. If you have a cigarette every thirty to ninety minutes during the day, you will only feel these withdrawal symptoms first thing in the morning or perhaps in the middle of the night.

Many smokers put off trying to quit because they fear the pain of withdrawal from nicotine. In reality, the *fear* of the pain of withdrawal is greater than the pain of withdrawal. Many smokers who work this program discover that withdrawal is little more than a minor inconvenience. "Get real," you may say. "I've heard what it's like." The truth is that the withdrawal from nicotine can be uncomfortable and may at times make you (and the people around you) wish you had never stopped smoking. However, nicotine withdrawal causes no serious illnesses, no major health problems, and no need for hospitalization. No one has ever died; had a seizure, stroke, or heart attack; or had to call 911 because of nicotine withdrawal. They just wanted it to be over. Now.

If you anticipate that withdrawal from nicotine will be a serious problem for you, don't worry. Medications are available to help; you can read about them in the next chapter. Before you use any of them, however, you should understand how *your* body and brain react to withdrawal from nicotine.

Most smokers find that they smoke only about 20 percent of their cigarettes to stay out of withdrawal; they smoke the rest either because (a) they like the "buzz" the cigarette gives; (b) they are using the cigarette to deal with uncomfortable feelings (such as anxiety, anger, or fear); or (c) the situation they are in just seems to call for a cigarette. Obviously, withdrawal medication will only help you replace the cigarettes you would use to combat withdrawal. The medications will not replace the other cigarettes you smoke: you can't use them to treat anxiety or anger, you can't use them to look sophisticated, and you can't blow smoke rings with them.

Therefore, before you decide to use medication to treat nicotine withdrawal, you must understand your own withdrawal very well.

✎ *Here are some of the signs and symptoms of withdrawal from nicotine. Which ones do you have?*

When I haven't had a cigarette in quite a while . . .

I begin to feel	And I begin to have
❑ irritable	❑ intense cravings to smoke
❑ short-tempered	❑ trouble concentrating
❑ a loss of self-control	❑ a short attention span
❑ restless	❑ trouble remembering things
❑ sweaty	❑ unreasonable fears
❑ spacey	❑ mood swings
❑ agitated	❑ trouble sleeping
❑ anxious	❑ abdominal cramps

I begin to feel	And I begin to have
❑ shaky	❑ headaches
❑ drowsy	❑ hunger pangs
❑ suspicious	❑ uncontrollable yawning
❑ talkative	❑ periods of confusion
❑ very excitable	❑ crying spells
❑ like yawning all the time	❑ frightening dreams

and _____

ADDICTIVE BEHAVIOR

The third characteristic of addictive chemicals is that they cause typical and consistent behaviors. We can understand these better by dividing them into drug-seeking behavior and dependent behavior.

Drug-Seeking Behavior

Individuals who become addicted to chemicals seek their chemicals and use them in characteristic ways. Certain behaviors are typical for certain drugs. For instance, consider how addicts obtain their drugs. Valium addicts usually get their prescriptions from several different doctors and have them filled at several different pharmacies. Crack cocaine addicts buy their drugs on the street. Physicians addicted to Demerol usually buy their own drugs, while nurses addicted to Demerol usually take vials of it from the hospital where they work. Underage smokers buy their cigarettes from convenience stores and cigarette machines, while adult smokers tend to buy theirs at grocery stores and tobacco shops.

Individuals develop consistent patterns in the way they use their chemicals as well. Heroin addicts use their heroin alone or with a group of other addicts. Alcoholics drink at bars, at home alone, or with a group of other alcoholics. Smokers also use cigarettes in characteristic ways. In fact, there are probably more addictive behaviors associated with smoking than with other addictive chemicals.

Consider some of your addictive behaviors. Ask yourself these questions:

- How and where do I buy my cigarettes?
- How do I open the carton?
- How do I open the pack?
- Do I handle the first cigarette from a pack in a special way?
- What do I do with the cigarette when I first take it out of the pack, before I light it?
- Do I light each cigarette in the same way?
- Is the first drag special in some way?
- Do I usually hold and handle the cigarette the same way?
- How do I tap off the ash?
- Do I puff on it in the same way most of the time?
- What unique things do I do with the smoke?
- What do I do as the cigarette burns down to the end?
- How do I usually put it out?
- What do I usually do with the cigarette butt?
- Where do I keep my cigarettes?
- Where do I keep my lighter or matches?
- Do I have special cigarettes for special occasions?
- When someone asks me for a cigarette, what do I do?
- *How do I smoke when I'm under stress?*

A cigarette is a splendid container for nicotine, but it is much more. Pure nicotine in the form of chewing gum is available, but very few people become addicted to it. Smoking involves much more than just nicotine. There are so many wonderful things to do with a cigarette! Cigarettes that make very little smoke have been developed too, but studies have shown that smokers do not like them. Another study showed that when smokers were allowed to smoke in a dark room where they could not see the smoke, they lost interest in smoking. It seems that not just the nicotine, but also the cigarette, the tobacco, the fire, and the smoke are all part of the addiction. Smokers seek nicotine, but they also want the package it comes in. And, as it turns out, there is no better way to get the nicotine into your system than by smoking a cigarette.

The Philip Morris Company, which makes and sells Marlboro and other brands of cigarettes, understands this well. Here is an excerpt from a report written for Philip Morris describing the proceedings of a company conference held in 1972:

> *The cigarette should be conceived not as a product but as a package. The product is nicotine. The cigarette is but one of many*

package layers. There is the carton, which contains the pack, which contains the cigarette, which contains the smoke. The smoke is the final package. The smoker must strip off all these package layers to get at that which he seeks. . . . Think of the cigarette pack as a storage container for a day's supply of nicotine. . . . Think of the cigarette as a dispenser for a dose unit of nicotine. . . . Think of a puff of smoke as the vehicle of nicotine. Smoke is beyond question the most optimized vehicle of nicotine and the cigarette the most optimized dispenser of smoke.

Cigarettes help you do so many things. For instance, they help you structure your day. You start the day with a cigarette, and you end it with a cigarette. The cigarette starts your coffee break and ends your lunch hour. You might hesitate to tell your co-workers, "I need a little time for myself right now, so please leave me alone," but you have no difficulty telling them, "I'm going outside for a smoke."

Smokers depend on cigarettes to help them structure their time and organize their day.

The cigarettes that help me structure my day are . . .

❑ the first one I have in the morning
❑ the last one I smoke at night
❑ the ones I have with meals
❑ the one I smoke at the end of my work day
❑ the one I have after sex
❑ the one I light up before I get started on a new task
❑ the ones I have with friends at lunch or on a break
❑ the ones I smoke during staff meetings
❑ the one I use as an excuse to stop talking with someone
❑ the one I smoke in order to get some "time out"

and _____

Automatic Smoking

In time, smoking becomes automatic. Certain situations trigger the desire to smoke, and you automatically reach for your cigarettes. Smoking is a complex act, yet eventually you learn to smoke without any thought at all. Have you ever lit a cigarette, taken a puff, and set it down in the ashtray only to discover that you had one smoldering there already? You took out the pack, removed a cigarette, picked up your lighter, lit the cigarette, and puffed on it—all automatically.

Many people react to the sound of the telephone ringing by reaching for a cigarette. They pick up the telephone with one hand and their pack of cigarettes with the other. As they begin the conversation, they put a cigarette in their mouth and light it. They can do this even while concentrating on the telephone call because they are smoking automatically.

Some people smoke automatically while watching television. They smoke one cigarette after another, never taking their eyes off the TV. They can pay attention to the TV show and smoke because they are smoking automatically.

Some people light up as soon as they get into their car. They light the cigarette as automatically as they put the key in the ignition, start the engine, and shift into gear.

Other people start to smoke the moment they walk out of their office or home. They do not even realize they are smoking, because they do it automatically.

Until you discover what your own automatic smoking behaviors are, you will continue to smoke automatically in certain situations, and cigarettes will continue to control your life. When you discover what the behaviors are, you will be able to change them.

After you quit smoking, you are still in danger of relapsing, however. If you do a lot of automatic smoking now, you will be at great risk of relapse when you are in certain situations. Now is the time to learn more about your automatic smoking behaviors. Here are some examples of automatic smoking.

I light a cigarette automatically . . .

❑ when I wake up in the morning
❑ when I get out of the shower
❑ when I walk out the door
❑ when I get into my car
❑ when I walk out of class
❑ when I feel angry
❑ when I hear the telephone ring
❑ at 5:00 P.M.

❏ when I sit down in front of the TV
❏ when I have a drink
❏ when I hear bad news
❏ after dinner
❏ after having sex
❏ before going to bed
❏ if I wake up during the night

and _____

Try this: tuck a business card into your cigarette package, and write down the time you smoke each cigarette all day today. (Smoke as much as you usually do; this is an exercise in becoming aware of when you smoke.) You will have to pause before smoking; this will interrupt your automatic smoking. Do this each day for a week, using a new card each day. Then look over all your cards or show them to someone else. What do you notice?

If this exercise does not appeal to you, consider a variation: each morning, write down on the card the times you *expect* to smoke a cigarette. During the day, put a check next to the time when you actually smoked one. You will discover how much you really know about when you smoke. This simple exercise can also help you make choices about smoking as you cut down.

Some things I discovered by keeping track of when I smoke are . . .
❏ I smoke at certain predictable times each day.
❏ I smoke in certain situations each day.
❏ I smoke in response to certain feelings.
❏ I smoke more than I thought I did.
❏ I smoke _____ "automatic" cigarettes each day.
❏ I don't like the feeling of being controlled by a cigarette.

and _____

Becoming *aware* of when you smoke is an important step in preventing automatic smoking from controlling you. You will soon be able to turn down many of these cigarettes, and smoke only part of many others, because you will be aware of each cigarette you smoke.

Smoking Rituals

When people do things in the same way again and again, so that it becomes the natural way to do things, they have created a ritual. Rituals and automatic behaviors have a lot in common. You might do a certain thing without really thinking about it (an automatic behavior) and when you do it, you do it the same way every time (a ritual). You do it in certain situations (a ritual) and you do it every time you are in that situation (an automatic behavior). You cannot seem to prevent yourself from doing it (an automatic behavior), but you do not really mind because you feel more comfortable and secure when you do it (a ritual).

You follow rituals at church. When you walk into the church you usually attend, you know what to expect. The hymns and prayers and surroundings are familiar. The minister greets you in the same way, and you know the order of the service. When you attend a different church for the first time, everything is unfamiliar and you feel less secure and less comfortable.

The familiarity of the rituals at church makes you feel welcome. You rely on them to help feel secure.

You have rituals in other areas of your life as well. You may have morning rituals: turn off the alarm, stretch, (smoke a cigarette?), use the toilet, do some exercises, shower, shave or put on makeup, get dressed, eat breakfast. You may have driving rituals: adjust the mirror, put the key in the ignition, start the car, tilt the steering wheel, (light a cigarette?), shift into gear, and drive to work. You may have similar rituals for your lunch hour, coffee break, meetings, and evenings out.

The real purpose of rituals is not to help you live and work more efficiently, but to help you feel more secure. Some people always put their right shoe on and tie it before they put on their left shoe. This is a helpful little ritual that gets them started on their day. Other people do it just the other way around. Both work just as well. The ritual is important because it helps the person feel in control as the day gets started, not because it matters which shoe goes on first.

Smokers incorporate cigarettes into many of their rituals. The morning ritual of most smokers, for example, includes one or two (or more) cigarettes. For some, the withdrawal from nicotine forces them to smoke before they even get out of bed. Others smoke their first cigarette on the toilet, while shaving or putting on makeup, or while drinking the first cup of coffee in the morning. The sequence tends to be personal, unique, and consistent from one day to the next.

My morning ritual includes these cigarettes:
- ❏ one before I get out of bed
- ❏ one right after getting out of bed
- ❏ one after showering
- ❏ one while using the toilet
- ❏ one while shaving or putting on makeup
- ❏ one while drinking coffee
- ❏ one while eating breakfast
- ❏ one while reading the newspaper
- ❏ one just before I leave for work

and _____

Over the years, you have developed rituals around your smoking, and like other rituals, they give you a sense of security. When your world feels out of control, at least you can control your cigarettes. When you do not know what to do, you can play with your cigarettes. When you are embarrassed, frightened, worried, tense, angry, or hurt, you can focus on your cigarettes and feel a little better.

The smoking ritual begins with choosing a brand and buying a pack or a carton. Most smokers stick with one brand. A very few will smoke any brand available, but most smokers choose the same brand every time. The ritual continues with where you carry them and how you open the pack, extract a cigarette, light it, smoke it, and put it out.

These smoking rituals are part of your drug-seeking behavior. By helping you feel better, they keep you controlled and ensure that you will continue to smoke. As long as you allow cigarettes to control you, you will never be able to quit smoking.

Of all the smoking rituals, the "opening-the-pack" ritual is particularly interesting. One man in a smoking cessation program, a former mechanic, reported that he always opened his cigarette pack from the bottom. This ritual started back in the days when he was working as a mechanic and didn't want the grease from his hands to get on the cigarette filter. When he was promoted to service manager, he continued to open his pack this way, even though his hands were always clean. Although his way of opening cigarette packs made sense when he was a mechanic, he continued with the ritual even when it no longer served a useful purpose.

A woman in the same group denied that she had any smoking rituals. "I'm not like that," she said. She agreed, however, to work on becoming more aware of automatic behaviors by tucking a business card into her cigarette pack and jotting down the time before she smoked each cigarette. (Have you tried this yet?)

She returned the next week and told the group, "I *do* have some smoking rituals. I couldn't carry the business card because I always remove the cellophane from the cigarette package, crumple it up, put it into the ashtray, light my cigarette, touch the end of it to the cellophane, and watch it melt." Once she was aware of doing this, she became aware of many of her other smoking rituals.

One man said that when he opens a new pack, he always takes out the first cigarette, turns it over, and puts it back in the pack—to be saved as the last cigarette. One woman said she takes the foil from each new pack and folds it into interesting shapes while she smokes the first cigarette from the pack. Another man said he always takes out the first cigarette of each pack by poking it up from the bottom. Still another demonstrated how he taps a cigarette out of the pack if he is giving it to a friend, but takes one out differently for himself.

The list of interesting and unique smoking rituals goes on and on. Recognizing your own smoking rituals will help you change these addictive smoking patterns. When you understand what you have been doing, you will begin to regain control of your life.

✎ *Start thinking about your own smoking rituals by answering the following questions. Record your answers in your journal.*

- How do I buy cigarettes?
- How do I carry them?
- How do I open a pack?

- How do I take out a cigarette?
- How do I light a cigarette?
- How do I hold a cigarette?
- How do I puff on a cigarette?
- How do I tap off the ash?
- How do I put it out?
- How do I throw it away?
- What other smoking rituals do I have?

You have developed social rituals around smoking as well. You gather with smoking friends around coffee and cigarettes, or drinks and cigarettes, or drugs and cigarettes—but always with cigarettes. It's like gathering around a campfire, with friends and closeness and warmth and the fire glowing. What a wonderful ritual! No wonder you've continued to smoke.

How many of your close friends are smokers? Do you look forward to sharing a cigarette with them? When you think about your non-smoking friends, do you feel something is missing from your relationship? Do you wish they smoked?

Do you know the brand each of your smoking friends smokes? Can you imitate their smoking mannerisms? Do you identify them as smokers? Can you imagine them without a cigarette? Do you think they can imagine *you* without a cigarette? Can you imagine yourself without a cigarette?

✎ *Finish the following two sentences on a separate sheet of paper.*

1. My smoking friends are . . .
2. Their typical smoking behaviors are . . .

Your smoking rituals have provided you with great relief from stress over the years—and these rituals have helped keep you addicted to cigarettes. In order to quit and stay quit, you will need to understand your smoking rituals and find other ways of dealing with stress.

After so many years of smoking, you now expect cigarettes to make you feel a certain way. You expect cigarettes to relieve you of stress, anxiety, boredom, and other uncomfortable feelings. And the cigarettes always deliver.

Cigarettes became your companions, always available, always nearby, always behaving just as expected, never disappointing. You've become loyal to your cigarettes just as your cigarettes have been loyal to you. You look forward to your cigarettes, plan for them, organize your time around them, and depend on them.

Cigarettes became a way of rewarding yourself for completing a task, solving a problem, or just making it through another day. You may have discovered that you expect a cigarette whenever you complete something, and your mind is on the cigarette all during the task. Perhaps you look forward to the cigarette that will give you some "time out" during your day or to the one you share with friends at lunch.

✎ *Which cigarettes do you most look forward to? List them in your journal.*

Now that you understand more about your drug-seeking behaviors, you will be better equipped to change them.

Dependent Behavior

When a chemical becomes more important to a person than personal values, that person has become "dependent" on the chemical. As a person's addiction progresses, the chemical becomes more important than family, employment, finances, friends, ethics, or self-respect.

Chemicals that become this important alter the way people think and feel: doctors call them "mind- and mood-altering chemicals." People don't become dependent on aspirin, even if they take it all the time for their arthritis, because it is not mind- or mood-altering. Mind- and mood-altering chemicals include alcohol, barbiturates, heroin, amphetamines, cocaine, marijuana—and tobacco. Some are more addictive than others, but they are *all* potentially addictive.

Cocaine, amphetamines, and heroin are such powerful drugs that people using them reach the end stages of addiction very quickly—often over just a few months of use. Alcohol is not as potent, and it takes most alcoholics many years to reach this point.

Cigarettes are different. Smokers can become just as addicted to cigarettes as heroin addicts to heroin but without ruining their lives, threatening their marriages, or jeopardizing their jobs. Wives do not tell their husbands, "Unless you quit smoking, I'm taking the kids and moving out!" Husbands do not keep their wives hidden at home so that the neighbors will not discover that they smoke. Parents do not send their children off to military school to keep them away from tobacco.

Any addict might spend the rent money on chemicals, but since a carton of cigarettes costs much less than one week's rent, most people do not suffer financially by being smokers. Our society accepts tobacco use (although less so today than a few years ago), and our government finances tobacco production and distribution. So even though smokers become dependent on cigarettes, their social lives are rarely destroyed because of it.

Many smokers are unable to go for more than an hour without smoking, even on the job. If they were addicted to another chemical, they would have to find a more flexible job—but most jobs permit frequent smoking breaks, or even permit smoking while working. Mechanics, construction workers, bartenders, receptionists, actors, and most self-employed people expect to be able to smoke while at work. (Can you imagine a job that would permit injecting amphetamines while at work?) So although cigarettes do become more important than some parts of your life, they will not seriously interfere with your life for many years.

Over the years, your smoking has become an integral part of your life. You may be upset to discover that smoking has become more important in many ways than your family, your friends, your job, or your finances. Certainly, very few smokers have literally abandoned their families in favor of cigarettes—but every day you choose to smoke instead of doing something else.

Did you ever excuse yourself at a party to step outside for a cigarette because you knew the hosts were nonsmokers? You chose cigarettes over your friends.

Did one of your children ever look up at you and say, "I wish you'd quit smoking," and you mumbled some excuse? You chose cigarettes over your family.

Did you ever smoke when you had the flu or bronchitis? You chose cigarettes over your health.

Did you change jobs when your company went smoke-free? You chose cigarettes over your job.

How important to you *are* your cigarettes?

Characteristics of Addictive/Dependent Smoking

Here are those nine characteristics of addiction (items 4 through 12) that were listed at the beginning of this chapter, but with "smoker" replacing "addict" and "smoking" or "cigarettes" now replacing "chemical":

4. The smoker is preoccupied or obsessed with smoking.
5. The smoker craves cigarettes.
6. The smoker rationalizes his or her smoking.
7. The smoker continues to smoke in spite of good reasons not to.
8. Cigarettes become more important than family, friends, job, ethics, or money.
9. The smoker who starts smoking again after a period of abstinence quickly resumes his or her previous patterns and number of cigarettes smoked.
10. The smoker sneaks and hides cigarettes.
11. The smoker chooses friends, jobs, and recreation that permit smoking, avoiding friends, jobs, and recreation that do not allow smoking.
12. Physical deterioration begins, but the smoker continues to smoke.

Do any of these dependency characteristics apply to you and your smoking?

Relapse Behaviors

One other important characteristic of addictive and dependent behaviors is that the addict tends to make many unsuccessful attempts to quit. Each attempt at quitting is prompted by something that seems important at the time, and the attempt at quitting may be a serious one. But because addictions are much more powerful than logic, the addicted person returns to using chemicals in spite of the many good reasons not to, and rationalizes the relapse.

Have you ever quit smoking for a day, a week, a month, or a year? What happened? Why did you start smoking again? How long did it take until you were smoking just as much as you did before? How did you feel after you relapsed? What did you tell people? What did you tell yourself?

Relapse is characteristic of all addictions, smoking included. Interestingly, the data show that people who have made several attempts at quitting are more successful at quitting and staying quit than people who have never tried to quit. This may be because such people are highly motivated to quit or because they learn a few more useful techniques each time they try. So if you have tried to quit before and relapsed, your chances of quitting this time are actually better than they were before.

✎ *Take this opportunity to recall some of the times you quit in the past. Record your thoughts in your journal.*

- The most recent time I tried to quit smoking was . . .
- I think I started again because . . .
- When I started again, I felt . . .
- Some other times I tried to quit smoking were . . .
- The similarities I notice are . . .

Most smokers would be able to fill up ten or twelve pages with failed attempts at quitting. Imagine how frustrating these repeated failures have been!

This program emphasizes *staying* quit, not quitting. Most smokers become angry and frustrated when they make a sincere attempt to quit and then relapse. By working this program, you can avoid these disappointments. Wait until you are really ready before you say "I've quit."

Your cigarette smoking satisfies the strict definition of addictive chemical use if you agree with these four statements:

1. I have developed *tolerance*. I smoke more than I once did.
2. I have *withdrawal signs* and *symptoms*. I experience them a little bit each morning, but they are more pronounced when I've tried to quit for a few days—smoking relieves the pain.
3. I have a characteristic set of *behaviors* associated with my smoking. They seem to be just about as important to me as the nicotine.
4. I am *dependent* on cigarettes. I have made my cigarettes more important than things in my life that were once very important.

Well, you're certainly not the first person to become addicted to tobacco. You've had lots of famous company over the years. Here is a little-known but true story about a famous tobacco addict.

Sigmund Freud is best known as the founder of psychoanalysis, today considered a branch of psychiatry. He was trained as a physician and specialized in neurology for many years. In his late thirties, he became interested in the function and development of the mind. He psychoanalyzed himself, wrote extensively, and probably made more contributions to the understanding of the mind than anyone before him.

Freud was addicted to cigars. He inhaled them and smoked about twenty each day. When he was thirty-eight, he had problems with an irritable heart; he was advised to quit smoking, but he could not. When he was sixty-seven, he developed cancer of the mouth and jaw, and over the next thirteen years had a total of thirty-three operations to control and repair the damage. When he was seventy-three, he made an attempt to quit smoking and stayed "clean" for only twenty-three days. When he was seventy-nine, he had to have an artificial jaw implanted, his own having been eaten away by cancer—but still he could not quit. At age eighty-one, he is said by his biographer to have been smoking "an endless series of cigars."

Earlier in his life, Freud used cocaine to treat his depression. He later decided that cocaine was too dangerous and had too many side effects, so he quit using it. In other words, *he could quit using cocaine, but he could not quit using tobacco.*

Here you have one of the most brilliant men of our time, unable to quit smoking. His intelligence was no match for his addiction. His tremendous insight into his character was no help either. This man probably had as great an understanding of the human mind as anyone before or since, but he was unable to apply it to himself. Because Freud never understood his addiction, it mutilated him.

Psychoanalysis has taught us much about the workings of the mind, and through analysis, many people have received help. But recovery from addictions requires a different approach—one based on accepting and understanding the addiction and developing new living skills. These will be your goals in the pages ahead.

An addiction is a chronic disease, like diabetes. It never really goes away, although it does go into remission. Like Freud, you will always be *addicted* to tobacco, but unlike him, you can become a *nonsmoker.* Even though you have been addicted, you do *not* have to keep smoking.

Right now, you are a smoker who is not smoking. (If you are smoking while you are reading this, you must be *highly* addicted.) When you have succeeded at this challenge, you will visualize yourself as a non-smoker. You will know deep inside that despite being addicted, you do not ever have to smoke again.

If you are like most smokers, you have quit on one or more occasions, but have started again. In other words, you *quit,* but you did not *stay* quit. The addiction remained within you. Once you started smoking again the addiction took control, and you soon resumed smoking in your previous pattern.

There is no adequate explanation for why addictions never go away. Even after twenty years of abstinence, the addiction will still be there, lurking, hiding, waiting for an opportunity to reemerge.

The tolerance goes into hiding, but it reappears with striking speed. If you start smoking after being abstinent for a long time, the first cigarette will make you light-headed, but by the fifth one, your tolerance will have completely returned.

The withdrawal goes into hiding, too, but comes back almost as quickly. If you smoke one cigarette after being abstinent for a long time and then stop, you will have a few relatively insignificant withdrawal symptoms. But if you smoke as little as one pack and then quit, you will have a long list of withdrawal signs and symptoms. And if you smoke for a week and then quit again, it will be as if you had never quit.

The addiction goes into remission, but it never goes away. You are never *cured* of an addictive disease. Understanding this and really accepting it are major parts of your recovery program. Accepting the addictive nature of tobacco and the fact that you have become addicted to it are the most important steps you can take toward a lifetime of freedom from cigarettes.

Having an addiction does not make you a bad person. Addiction to tobacco is a disease, like diabetes or high blood pressure. You did not plan to become addicted when you smoked your first cigarette. If you had known you were going to have this much trouble quitting, you probably would never have started smoking.

The past cannot be changed. There is no point in being hard on yourself for past errors. Rather, it is time to accept your past, flaws and all, and move on to the future with the confidence that you can become more like the person you want to be. The person you are today is the sum of all the events of your life, the ones you would be glad to repeat as well as the ones you would prefer not to. This includes your addiction to smoking. It is part of who you are. You may be disappointed or angry or resentful about the past, but you cannot change it. One of the goals of this program is to show you how you can accept who you are and go about making your future brighter.

The projects ahead in this book are designed to help you focus on your addiction and how it has affected you in ways you cannot now imagine. You will discover that your smoking addiction has affected nearly every part of your life, and that quitting (and staying quit) will require profound lifestyle and personal changes. This challenge of quitting smoking will not be easy. But in the process you will discover much about yourself and you will become more like the person you want to be.

This is a journey, not a destination. Quitting is just one point on the journey. You should not try to quit today, or tomorrow. In fact, you will not even be asked to reduce the number of cigarettes you smoke for several chapters yet, and you will never be asked to switch to a brand with low nicotine or low tar. When you cut down on the number of cigarettes you smoke each day, and when you quit entirely, you will have reached a goal *you have set for yourself.*

If you are working this program with a group, you may find that some of the group members are cutting down as they work on these projects. Even without being told to, they may find themselves choosing not to smoke, leaving their cigarettes at home, or crushing out a cigarette after two or three puffs. They may soon discover that up to half of the cigarettes they smoke are not all that important to them. Has this happened to you too?

Some people prefer an "all-or-nothing" approach. They cannot cut down, so they choose to stop all at once. They work the projects in this book, set a Quit Day, and stop.

Others experience an emotional crisis that releases them. One woman came to her group and broke into tears. "I'm a failure," she sobbed. "Everyone else is cutting down but me. I can't do anything right. I quit alcohol and drugs two years ago, but I can't quit smoking. And now I realize I was never sober at all. I was still using a drug—tobacco! I'll *never* be able to quit!" The next week she was all smiles. "I went home that night," she told the group, "and threw away my cigarettes, and I haven't had one since."

You can cut down bit by bit, or quit all at once. It makes no difference. You can quit today or tomorrow, next week, next month, or next year. Success is not measured by *when* you quit, but by your comfort in the role of a nonsmoker. The goal of this book is to help you quit and *stay* quit, and to be happy with yourself. If you need to, you may smoke for another week, another month, or another year.

Do not actually quit until you are really ready. Each time you quit for a while and then start smoking again, you get more frustrated and angry with yourself. You have plenty of frustration in your life as it is—you do not need any more. If you quit before you are well prepared, you will start smoking again. Be well prepared first.

Diligent work on the projects in this book will help you become prepared; sharing with others who are working to improve their health through quitting also helps. This is an *investment* of time and effort, an investment in yourself and your future. Your gains in this program will be in direct proportion to the amount of time and effort you invest in it.

After you have smoked your last cigarette, you may be tempted to put this book away, satisfied that you have reached your goal. But remember: the goal is to quit and *stay* quit. The real work begins when you put out your last cigarette. Continue with this book so you can consolidate your gains, learn how to deal with life without smoking, and strengthen your resolve for the challenges ahead.

Tobacco and cigarettes are addicting. You are addicted to cigarettes. And soon, you will be a nonsmoker. For having stuck with the program this far, *Congratulations!* You are on your way to a life released from the tyranny of addiction to cigarettes.

4

Medications for Treating Withdrawal from Nicotine

If you are physically dependent on nicotine, you will experience withdrawal symptoms when you quit smoking. You may become irritable and tense; you may have trouble sleeping, have difficulty concentrating, or have mood swings. These symptoms are often the reason smokers give up their efforts to quit smoking, and the fear of withdrawal symptoms is one reason many smokers never even try to quit. Now that excellent medications to treat withdrawal are available, there is no reason for you to suffer.

There are five medications currently approved for treating nicotine withdrawal symptoms: four are nicotine replacement products, and the fifth is bupropion.

Nicotine gum (Nicorette) is not a gum; it is a resin to which nicotine is bound. When you chew it, nicotine dissolves in your saliva and is absorbed through the tissues inside your mouth. When used as part of a treatment program, it improves the chances for success; however, it is not very effective unless used along with some form of counseling.

There are several advantages to nicotine gum:

- You control the dose yourself; when you experience nicotine withdrawal symptoms, you can chew a piece of nicotine gum to relieve the symptoms.
- You can give your system a quick jolt of nicotine to relieve withdrawal symptoms by chewing rapidly, which raises the nicotine level in your blood very quickly.

- When you are ready to reduce your nicotine dose, you can use the gum to taper off gradually.
- The gum comes in a convenient plastic blister package and is available in pharmacies without a prescription.

However, there are a number of disadvantages to nicotine gum:

- Chewing gum is just not possible at times.
- Chewing a lot of this gum can cause soreness in your jaw and neck muscles.
- You must keep the saliva in your mouth to absorb the nicotine. If you swallow frequently, you will absorb less nicotine and you may get an upset stomach.
- Because the gum has an unpleasant taste, some people are tempted to chew regular gum with it; you should not do this. Anything that makes your mouth even slightly acidic (coffee, fruit juice, cola, fruit-flavored gum, and so on) prevents the nicotine from being absorbed.

There are two ways to use nicotine gum. One way is to chew enough gum to completely eliminate nicotine withdrawal symptoms, and then gradually decrease the number of pieces you use each day over several weeks. With this method, you start by chewing a piece of gum every 30 to 60 minutes, chewing until you taste the peppery flavor of the gum, and then parking the gum next to your cheek for a while. After 20 or 30 minutes you will have sucked all the nicotine out of that piece, and you discard it.

The alternative way is to use just enough nicotine gum to relieve nicotine withdrawal symptoms when they occur. First thing in the morning, you may need one or two pieces; at other times, half a piece or even a quarter of a piece of gum may be enough. Chew the gum very rapidly to mimic the shot of nicotine a cigarette gives you; as soon as the immediate withdrawal symptoms are gone (usually in less than two minutes), discard the gum.

The nicotine patch (Habitrol, Nicoderm, ProStep, and Nicotrol) approximately doubles the success rate of whatever else you are doing to quit smoking. All four brands of the patch contain nicotine, but there are differences in their delivery systems, the amount of nicotine per patch, and the amount and rate at which the nicotine is delivered to you.

There are two particular advantages of the patch over the gum:

- The patches send pure nicotine across your skin and into your system at a steady rate all day long. This avoids the swings in nicotine blood levels that contribute to addiction,
- You stick a patch on your skin in the morning—anywhere it will stick is fine—and forget about it.

There are several disadvantages to the patch, though:

- At most, there are only three possible doses; cutting the patch to change the dose is not a good idea because some nicotine may leak out and the patch will not stick well.
- The patch causes skin irritation in up to half of patients using it.
- It takes about two hours for the nicotine level in your system to rise after first putting the patch on; therefore, pulling it off at night is not a good idea for most people.
- When you feel the urge to smoke, rubbing the patch does no good at all; it is designed to give you a steady dose of nicotine and does not give you a "rush" like a cigarette does.
- You should not smoke while wearing the patch.

Most of the brands come in several sizes. Put a patch on your arm, flank, or stomach in the morning after bathing; the next morning, take it off, bathe, and put a new patch on in a different spot to reduce skin irritation. Start with the largest patch if you smoke more than 30 cigarettes a day and if you start smoking within five minutes of waking up. (Very heavy smokers may need two patches at once, or a patch and gum together.) Start with a smaller patch if you smoke less or if you usually wait an hour or more after waking up before smoking your first cigarette. You can drop from a large patch to a smaller one after a week or two. You can discuss this with your doctor, dentist or pharmacist.

The nicotine nasal spray (Nicotrol NS) shoots a measured dose of nicotine into the nose, where it is rapidly absorbed. The spray improves quit rates by relieving withdrawal, but it irritates the nose and may be more addictive than the patch.

The nicotine inhaler (Nicotrol Inhaler) looks like a cigarette holder; instead of putting a cigarette on the end, you place a porous cartridge containing nicotine inside the holder. Every time you suck on the inhaler, some of the nicotine (in vapor form) fills your mouth.

Bupropion (Zyban) is as effective at reducing nicotine withdrawal symptoms as the patch or the gum, although it does not contain nicotine. Bupropion raises the level of neurotransmitter chemicals in the brain that affect withdrawal and craving symptoms. Bupropion can reduce or eliminate the weight gain that often troubles people when they quit smoking, and can improve depressed mood.

The advantages of bupropion are that it relieves withdrawal symptoms, relieves craving symptoms, reduces or eliminates weight gain, improves depressed mood, and has no addictive properties.

Bupropion, however, can cause dry mouth and insomnia, and people with seizure disorders, anorexia, or bulimia should not use it.

The standard dose of bupropion for smoking cessation is one tablet (150 mg), twice a day, for seven to twelve weeks. Some people no longer need it after just a few weeks, and some do better if they take it for several months.

Bupropion is prescription-only, so if you think it might help you, ask your healthcare provider about it.

Will medication help you quit smoking? Nicotine replacement and Zyban have helped many smokers quit, but many people have failed because they put too much faith in these medications alone. Quitting smoking requires a personal commitment to change. Very few people can simply swallow a pill, and then toss their cigarettes away and never smoke again.

If you think that medication might help you, discuss it with your healthcare provider. But remember: no medication is going to solve your problems for you—only you can do that.

5

Taking the First Step To
Freedom from Smoking

When people become dependent on a chemical, whether that chemical is heroin, alcohol, marijuana, or tobacco, the chemical becomes part of their lives—and can become the most important part. Heroin or cocaine addicts spend the majority of every day thinking about their chemical, planning to obtain some, getting it, using it, and recuperating from it. The chemical becomes more important than money, time, friends, family, self-respect, the future, or even life itself. They are obsessed with their chemical, and they will take time to eat, sleep, or have sex only when they know they can get their chemical.

You probably do not think your cigarette smoking habit is *that* bad—and in many ways, you are right. Heroin dealers, suppliers, and users kill in order to protect their territory and products; you have probably not killed someone over a pack of cigarettes. Cocaine addicts frequently spend $200 a day on their addiction; you might not spend that much in two months on cigarettes. Alcoholics who live in a "dry" town think nothing of driving to the next county or the next state to get alcohol; you do not usually go to such extremes to get cigarettes.

Or do you?

You *do* think about cigarettes a lot. If you leave your house in a hurry, don't you always check your pockets or purse to be sure your cigarettes are there? If you had to sit in the nonsmoking section of a restaurant because the smoking section was full, would you think twice before accepting a table? Have you ever chosen to take two plane flights instead of a long nonstop flight so you could get off the plane to smoke? If you are at a party in the home of a nonsmoker, do you find yourself eyeing the weather (so you won't get wet if you duck outside for a smoke)?

✎ *What* are *the most extreme things you have ever done in order to smoke? Write them out on a separate sheet of paper.*

- The most extreme thing I ever did to obtain cigarettes was . . .
- The most extreme thing I ever did for a light was . . .
- The farthest I ever drove to get a cigarette was . . .
- The most I ever paid for a pack of cigarettes was . . .
- If cigarettes were illegal, there are times I would have paid as much as _____ for one cigarette.

A heroin addict might use heroin four or five times a day; a cocaine addict might use cocaine two or three times a day. But if you are a two-pack-a-day smoker, you use your chemical *forty times a day.* Therefore, more of your daily activities are associated with chemical use than a heroin addict's or a cocaine addict's. There are very few things you do that are *not* in some way associated with smoking. You smoke from the first thing in the morning until the last thing at night, and a cigarette accompanies you nearly everywhere.

- Do you need a cigarette before your feet hit the floor in the morning?
- Do you absolutely need a cigarette with that first cup of coffee?
- Do you take a cigarette with you to the bathroom?
- Do you smoke while you drive to work?
- Does the sight of your office trigger the need for a cigarette?
- When the telephone rings, do you reach for your cigarettes even before you reach for the receiver?
- Do you always smoke during your coffee break?
- As the pressures mount, does your desire to smoke also increase?
- On the way home, does a cigarette help relieve the stress?
- Do you smoke before, during, and after dinner?
- Do you smoke while watching TV, playing with the kids, doing your taxes, working on the car, sewing on buttons, or talking on the phone?

- Do you usually want a cigarette after having sex?
- Do you finish the day off with a cigarette before going to sleep?
- Do you want a cigarette right now?

✎ I usually smoke a cigarette while . . .

Can you think of a situation you *never* smoke in? Are there any?

- Have you ever smoked while taking a bath or shower?
- Have you ever smoked in a swimming pool or Jacuzzi?
- Did you smoke while you were in the hospital awaiting surgery?
- Did you smoke in the clean, fresh air of the mountains?
- Have you ever smoked while filling up your car with gas?
- Have you ever had asthma, bronchitis, or pneumonia and could barely breathe—but you smoked anyway?
- Did you ever smoke while reading about or watching a TV show about the dangers of smoking?
- Did you smoke after hearing about a friend or relative who had just had a heart attack or been diagnosed with cancer?

✎ The most unbelievable place or time I ever smoked was . . .

Cigarettes have infiltrated their way into every aspect of your life, into the fabric of your existence. There is scarcely any situation in which you have *never* smoked.

Cigarettes manipulate you unmercifully. They tell you where you will go and how long you will stay, how to spend your money, whom you will talk to, where you will eat, and how far from home you can go. How does it feel to be manipulated by a four-inch piece of compost? It controls you more than any person ever did or ever will. It controls you more than your supervisor, your banker, the IRS, or the government. If you could control the stock market the way cigarettes control you, you could retire right now. Right under your nose, cigarettes have been exploiting you for . . . for how many years? And how many more years do you intend to allow this to go on?

Let's say you were late this morning. You missed breakfast because you had to hurry. You were tied up over lunch, too, and with all the stress, you smoked a bit more heavily than usual. It is now four o'clock, and things have quieted down a bit. You notice that you are hungry, and you also want a cigarette. You pull out your crush-proof box and discover it is . . . EMPTY! You check your pockets or purse and find— six quarters, seven dimes, and eight nickels (that's $2.60).

What will you spend the money on? Food to satisfy your growling stomach, or cigarettes to satisfy your addiction?

✎ *You can put your answer here:* _____

Isn't that incredible?

So even though cigarettes may not have the glamour of cocaine, the intensity of amphetamines, or the thrill of LSD, you *have* become dependent on them. You never intended to become addicted—no addict does. You wish you did not have to quit—no addict wants to. With every addiction, it is the current and potential consequences of the addiction that convince the addict to stop using.

Drugs differ, but addiction recovery varies little. Recovery requires acceptance and personal change, and for *you* to recover from tobacco addiction will require that you thoroughly understand, believe, admit, and accept how intensely your cigarette smoking has controlled, manipulated, and nearly destroyed you. If you fall short of complete acceptance, you risk returning to smoking. The moment you wonder *Perhaps I can smoke just one* is the moment your recovery stops and your relapse begins. But when you earnestly take this first step, you are on your way to a new freedom, a new life—one free of dependence on cigarettes.

This book will help you reach that new freedom.

Let's continue this painful but necessary self-examination by identifying the times when you feel that you really need a cigarette.

TIMES I WANT A CIGARETTE

When you set out to answer the question *When do I want to smoke?* it seems like the answer is *All the time.* But it is *not* all the time; it is many, many, specific times. There are so many of them, though, that they run together, and it *seems* as if it's "all the time." A drumroll appears to be a continuous sound, but it is really many individual taps so close together that they cannot be distinguished. Like a drumroll, there are so many times that you smoke, your smoking seems to be continuous. After all, if you smoke two packs (forty cigarettes) a day, and if you puff eleven times on each cigarette, you use a cigarette and its nicotine 440 times each day. If you have smoked for twenty years, that would mean 440 puffs a day, 365 days a year, for 20 years. That comes to over three million puffs. That means over three million opportunities to connect smoking with your daily activities.

✎ A time I really want a cigarette is . . .

Now, do two things with this information: become more detailed, and examine what occurred just prior to it. Becoming more detailed (as you did in the first chapter of this book with your reasons for wanting to quit) will make this a personal motivator, and tracing it back in time will show you where the desire to smoke comes from.

✎ A detail:

✎ What led up to this time when I wanted a cigarette:

Here are some examples from other people's lives. Which ones apply to you?

- *A time I really want a cigarette is in the morning*—
  - when I first wake up
  - when I wake up on a workday
  - when I wake up on the weekend
  - when I wake up grumpy
  - when I wake up in a good mood
  - when I wake up healthy
  - when I wake up sick

- *A time I really want a cigarette is when I have a cup of coffee*—
  - at home in the morning
  - at the office
  - at lunch
  - while playing cards

  - with dessert at a restaurant
  - with a client
  - because I'm early for an appointment

- *A time I really want a cigarette is when I'm stuck in traffic—*
  - in the morning on the way to work
  - on the way home from work
  - and I'm late
  - and I've had a bad day
  - and I'm in a hurry

- *A time I really want a cigarette is after a meal—*
  - when they bring the coffee
  - when they bring the dessert, and before they bring the coffee
  - actually, I start wanting a cigarette when I'm ordering dessert, and I'm anticipating eating it, drinking coffee, and smoking a cigarette
  - now that I think about it, as I'm eating my meal, I start looking forward to finishing it off with a cigarette
  - you know, I probably start wanting a cigarette just after I put out the one I was smoking before we started to eat

- *A time I really want a cigarette is when someone criticizes me.*
- *A time I really want a cigarette is when I'm reading a book.*
- *A time I really want a cigarette is after having sex.*
- *A time I really want a cigarette is while shaving in the morning.*
- *A time I really want a cigarette is when I'm relaxing.*
- *A time I really want a cigarette is when I'm nervous.*
- *A time I really want a cigarette is when I see someone else smoking.*
- *A time I really want a cigarette is when I haven't had one in an hour.*

and _____

A college student who completed this program once described how she always smoked a cigarette while walking from one class to another. She said her smoking trigger was walking outside and seeing all the cigarette butts on the ground where people had tossed them on their way in. She traced this smoking trigger back in time:

- I want a cigarette when I see all the cigarette butts on the ground outside the door.
- I want a cigarette when I open the door to leave the building.
- I want a cigarette while walking down the hall to leave the building.
- I want a cigarette as soon as I leave the classroom.

- I want a cigarette when I notice that the class period is nearly over.
- I want a cigarette when the class begins and I know I won't be able to smoke for an hour.
- *Actually,* I really want a cigarette when I toss away the one I was smoking on the way into the building onto the ground with all the others.

✎ Another thing that triggers my desire to smoke is . . .

You can see that with some effort, you can find half a dozen components to each trigger. You will begin to understand how you depend on cigarettes to deal with pressure, boredom, frustration, anger, loneliness, fear, anxiety, and many other stresses. You will find out which situations trigger your desire to smoke, and you will discover how your need for a cigarette can grow even when you are unaware of it.

You may not want to sit down and do this project. As you find more and more things in your life that you associate with smoking, you may begin to feel discouraged and wonder if you will *ever* be able to quit and stay quit. *Yes, you will be able to!* This book will help you reach your goal, so don't stop working now. Find a new smoking trigger each day, write it in your journal, and you will be a bit closer to quitting and staying quit.

✎ I always think about smoking when I see . . .

Keep it up. Don't be afraid to face the pain of realizing how many times and in how many ways your world has been influenced by cigarettes.

If you think this is a lot of work, you're right. It is. But understanding your smoking triggers will allow you to make plans to deal with them. If you ignore your triggers, you will remain at their mercy.

✎ One thing I cannot imagine doing without a cigarette is . . .

Even after you complete this chapter, you will continue to uncover new smoking associations for a long time. One night you might see Clint Eastwood in *The Good, the Bad and the Ugly* on the late movie.

Old Clint gets off his horse, grimaces, pulls a cheroot out of his pocket, bends down to the fire, and lights it. Suddenly, you notice your hand in your pocket, searching for a cigarette pack that hasn't been there for months. Quick! Get out your journal and write, "A time I really want a cigarette is when I see Clint Eastwood looking macho with a cigarette."

✎ A movie star I associate with smoking is . . .

✎ Smoking makes me feel . . .

Or perhaps you will be on vacation, relaxing on the beach at Cozumel. You see an attractive newcomer climb out of the pool, pick up a towel and a drink, and light up a cigarette. You suddenly realize that *you* want one too. Reach into your beach bag for a scrap of paper and scribble, "A time I really want a cigarette is when I see someone I'm attracted to light up a cigarette."

✎ A place I associate with smoking is . . .

✎ I am attracted to people who smoke because . . .

You might be bowling with your team in the finals of the league championship. It's all up to you in the final frame—and you leave a 4-7-10 split. You miss it and your team loses by two pins. There is a pack of cigarettes on the table, and you reach for it. Suddenly, you develop a new insight, and you realize, "A time I really want a cigarette is when I am disappointed in myself." Write it down!

✎ A leisure activity I associate with smoking is . . .

✎ I want a cigarette when I feel . . .

If you are working this program with a group, bring your insights to them and share what you have learned about yourself. You may hear about some smoking triggers that also apply to you, but that you were unaware of. You will get lots of encouragement to keep at it, and you will give this same encouragement to others.

You may discover recurring themes, such as the following:

- Sometimes I feel out of control, but a cigarette is something I can control.
- I always seem to want a cigarette after completing something.
- I need a cigarette when I get taken advantage of.
- I smoke when I have to ask a favor of someone.
- I reach for a cigarette when I anticipate a conflict.
- I really don't like myself very much, and when I screw up, I smoke a cigarette, almost like I'm punishing myself.
- I reward myself with a cigarette when I've done something I'm proud of.

Aren't you amazed at how cunning, baffling, and powerful your addiction to smoking is? Can you now see how tobacco has controlled you?

✎ Today, something that made me want to smoke was . . .

Each day is a new opportunity to learn more about yourself. You may have picked up this book solely with the intention of quitting smoking. You will discover, however, that your recovery from smoking addiction can be the route to learning more about yourself.

6

Attitudes about Smoking I

Having invested this much time and effort in understanding your smoking, chances are good that your *attitudes* about smoking have changed.

Your attitude about something includes your opinions, your feelings, and your expectations. Your attitudes are products of your previous experiences, what others have told you, and your fantasies about the future. Attitudes influence behavior: what you believe predicts what you will do.

Cigarettes

1. What was your attitude about cigarettes before you ever started to smoke? Here are some examples:

   - They were a "grown-up" thing. I looked up to the older kids who smoked.
   - My parents always warned me never to smoke and made me frightened of cigarettes.
   - I didn't like them because the smell of stale smoke was always around my house when I was growing up.

✎ My attitude . . .

2. What was your attitude about cigarettes soon after you started smoking? Here are some examples:

   - Cigarettes were a ticket of admission to the "in" crowd. When my friends got together, they all had cigarettes.

- I always felt guilty when I had cigarettes, and I hid them from my parents.
- Finding ways to get cigarettes was a challenge—getting the money, buying them, hiding them. The rest of my life was pretty dull, and cigarettes made it more interesting.

✎ My attitude . . .

3. What was your attitude about cigarettes just before you started this program? Here are some examples:

- I still liked smoking, but I had started hating cigarettes. Does that make any sense? I guess I was realizing that they were controlling me, and that I no longer had the choice to smoke or not to smoke.
- I knew I should quit. Every time I'd buy a pack (I had stopped buying them in cartons), I'd feel guilty. It even got to where I would look around to see if anyone was watching me when I bought them.
- I'd read plenty about the dangers of smoking, so I knew that cigarettes were bad for you.

✎ My attitude . . .

4. What is your attitude about cigarettes *today?* Here are some examples:

- Cigarettes have become a political tool and an economic necessity. They'll never be restricted, even if everyone in North Carolina and Kentucky gets cancer.
- If some people want to kill themselves by smoking, that's their business. I want to quit.
- Cigarettes are addicting. A person would have to be a certified idiot to start smoking today.

✎ My attitude . . .

Smoking

1. What was your attitude about smoking before you ever started to smoke? Here are some examples:

- Smoking cigarettes meant you were daring and thought for yourself and could take charge. In any crowd of kids, if only one kid was smoking, that kid was the leader.
- Smoking intrigued me. After all the horror stories everyone told me about smoking, I figured there must be something terrific about it that they all wanted to keep for themselves.
- I thought smoking was a smelly, disgusting habit.

✎ My attitude . . .

2. What was your attitude about smoking soon after you started smoking? Here are some examples:

- Actually, I thought smoking was stupid. I coughed a lot, and I didn't really like the way cigarettes tasted.
- I liked the light-headed feeling I got right from the first. The feeling was great, but I felt guilty whenever I smoked.
- When I started smoking, I became part of the crowd. Smoking was sort of required to be "in." Pretty soon, I was smoking all the time, and I liked it a lot.

✎ My attitude . . .

3. What was your attitude about smoking just before you started this program? Here are some examples:

- Oh, I still liked smoking. If I could have figured out how to smoke in control, I would have. Smoking has been my greatest pleasure.
- I was stupid to have started smoking in the first place. I should have known better. It was getting to be too much for me to handle, and when I decided to quit, it was a relief. Still, though, it took me several months to get around to doing anything about it. I don't know why—I really wanted to quit.
- I was really hooked. I couldn't even go all night without getting up to smoke a cigarette. I had never realized I could get so hooked. It sort of snuck up on me, and suddenly I realized I'd been hooked for years. That was pretty scary.

✎ My attitude . . .

4. What is your attitude about smoking *today?* Here are some examples:

- I wish some scientist would figure out how I can smoke just when I want to, instead of when I need to.
- Smoking is a disgusting habit and a compulsive addiction. Why I continue to smoke is beyond me.
- I understand now that I've become addicted to smoking. Smoking is without a doubt the stupidest thing I've ever done in my life.

✎ My attitude . . .

Smokers

1. What was your attitude about smokers before you ever started to smoke? Here are some examples:

- People who smoked were the leaders. They were in charge and they knew what they were doing. They were independent-minded, and I looked up to them.
- My parents and family all told me smokers were foolish, degenerate people who misused their bodies and wasted their money. But I was really curious, and not all the things they said about smokers really made sense. I was attracted to smokers, but at the same time, I was cautious.
- My parents both smoked, and I loved them, but I hated their smoking. I don't think I thought of people as "smokers" or "non-smokers," although I was always aware of when people smoked around me. When people smoked, they paid less attention to me and tended to be careless and sloppy.

✎ My attitude . . .

2. What was your attitude about smokers soon after you started smoking? Here are some examples:

- I was eager to join the kids who knew "where it was at." Becoming a smoker was part of that. All my friends were smokers, and we usually smoked the same brand too.
- After I started smoking, I discovered that about 80 percent of what my parents had told me about smokers was right. The other 20 percent was still plenty intriguing. All the exciting people I

met, it seemed, were smokers. I thought most nonsmokers were pretty dull.

- When I started to smoke, I quickly forgot all that stuff about how I didn't like my folks smoking. I joined the smoking crowd, and felt okay about it.

✎ My attitude . . .

3. What was your attitude about smokers just before you started this program? Here are some examples:

- At that time, I had done a lot of thinking about smokers. By and large, I felt, smokers (myself included) were pretty self-centered people. Smokers never care who breathes in their smoke, who has to clean up their ashtrays, or who has to pick up their cigarette butts.
- By the time I was ready to quit, I really wasn't paying too much attention to other smokers. I did notice that a lot of smokers had quit, though.
- I didn't care much what was happening to other smokers. I don't even remember discussing it much with anyone else. I knew I needed to quit, and that was all that was important.

✎ My attitude . . .

4. What is your attitude about smokers *today?* Here are some examples:

- Whether smokers are self-centered or not is not the question. Smokers have as much right to smoke as nonsmokers have not to smoke.
- I admire people who have successfully quit smoking, and I hope I will be able to also.
- I'd guess most of them are pretty miserable.

✎ My attitude . . .

The Future

1. What was your attitude about the future when you were young? On the next page are some examples.

- Simple: The world was my oyster, waiting to be cracked open. I was going to do great things and be important, and no one could stand in my way.
- I never thought much about the future. I figured things would pretty much fall into place for me. I'd get a job, get married, and all that sort of thing.
- I was never very worried about the future. I did pretty well in school, and I figured I would succeed at something. My parents were really supportive and always encouraged me without being too pushy.

✎ My attitude . . .

2. What was your attitude about the future just before you started this program? Here are some examples:

- I felt stuck. I was in a rut, getting nowhere. I was pretty discouraged about the future.
- I'd been at the same job for years and years, and I figured I'd still be there when I retired.
- I became pretty frightened when I discovered I was hooked and couldn't quit. I was afraid I was going to get emphysema or cancer or have a heart attack.

✎ My attitude . . .

3. What is your attitude about the future *today?* Here are some examples:

- I don't know. I'm still smoking, though not as much as I once was.
- I'm optimistic. This program looks like something I can stick with.
- My future is well planned. I want to quit smoking so I can enjoy it. What's the sense in working all my life and then dying from lung cancer?

✎ My attitude . . .

You will have an opportunity to observe the changes in your attitudes toward cigarettes, smoking, smokers, and the future. Both Parts II and III of this book have an "attitudes" chapter.

Questions and Answers I

Here are some questions I have been asked in the past. Perhaps some of them have occurred to you as well.

Did you ever smoke?

A lot of people ask me that question. First, let me say that therapists do not have to be former smokers in order to help you quit smoking. Now, I doubt that they would have much credibility if they are *current* smokers, but therapists who have never smoked can still successfully guide you to discovering solutions for your addiction.

And, yes, I used to smoke. When I quit smoking, there were no effective professional treatments for nicotine addiction, there was no Smokers Anonymous or Nicotine Anonymous, there were no non-smoking AA meetings (to my knowledge), and no books like this. Most people who have quit smoking have done so completely on their own or by following the advice of a doctor, friend, or family member. This book, and the support of a group, will make your journey to recovery easier.

Do I have to quit now? I'm scared.

No, you don't. In this program, each person sets his or her own goals and Quit Day. Whether the day you finish your last cigarette is today, tomorrow, or sometime next year is unimportant. Keep working with the material in this book, and you will achieve success in your own time.

Will the Quit and Stay Quit program work for me?

Do you want it to? No treatment method is foolproof. Most programs report a 30 to 50 percent "success" rate (meaning total abstinence from smoking for twelve months after completing treatment). Since most smokers seeking professional help are highly motivated and have selected a program they believe will work, this is a pretty dismal rate of success. I have run an intensive smoking cessation program, and it did no better than 50 percent success either. Why? We just have not yet discovered methods that are highly successful. I believe we will in time. Meanwhile, any method that works should be encouraged. This program is self-guided and relatively cheap (this book costs less than a week's worth of cigarettes) and has proved successful *for people who invest effort in it.* At the University of Texas Medical School at Houston, where I am a faculty member, we are doing research to discover better methods of treating nicotine dependence. Our findings will be reflected in improvements to this book.

Why do you think this program will work for me when all the other programs I've tried have not?

I encourage smokers to try any method they think will work, even if the method has no scientific validity (such as injections into your nose, staples in your ears, or pills to make you dislike tobacco). If it works for *you,* I'm all for it. Research shows that most successful quitters make many unsuccessful attempts at quitting, but with each effort, the cumulative success increases. This probably means that with each effort to quit, the smoker learns a little more, gets a little closer, or becomes more motivated. Eventually, the smoker quits for good.

Also, we must remember that all addictions are characterized by relapses and remissions. That is simply the nature of addictive illnesses. "Relapse" does not mean "failure"; it means that the addictive disease took hold again.

Sure, this program can work for you. Your success will be directly proportional to the amount of effort you invest in it. If you browse through these pages or read the text but fail to work the exercises, you will not get much out of it. If you keep your efforts a secret in order to surprise someone with your achievement (or to avoid embarrassment in case you can't quit), you will be reducing your chances for success. Invest time and effort in this program, make commitments to those you love, join up with a group of other smokers who are working the program, and your chances of success will be greatly improved.

A friend of mine had hypnosis and quit after one session. That certainly seems a lot easier than struggling through all these exercises. Maybe I should try hypnosis.

If you think hypnosis will work, by all means try it. I support the use of any method of smoking cessation that works. Many are no more effective than a placebo; but the goal is to quit smoking, and if a placebo works, that's fine with me.

I have been chewing a few pieces of Nicorette gum every day for about six months. It seems to help. Is this a problem?

Probably not. While we know that large amounts of nicotine can cause damage to your body, the amount contained in two or three pieces of Nicorette will not hurt you.

Be aware, though, that nicotine maintenance (which is what you are describing) is not the same as recovery. Even the small amount of nicotine you are using affects your thinking, your moods, and your feelings. I suggest you wean yourself off it.

Someone told me to switch to a low-tar brand. Is that a good idea?

"Nicotine fading" is recommended by some authorities. I do not recommend it. Research shows that when smokers of high-nicotine cigarettes were given low-nicotine cigarettes, they smoked more cigarettes, smoked more of each cigarette, and held the smoke in their lungs longer. Their nicotine levels stayed about the same on the low-nicotine cigarettes as they had been on the high-nicotine cigarettes. In the process, they subjected themselves to more carbon monoxide, and possibly more carcinogens. In addition, since they actually smoked more, they would have spent more money if they had been buying the cigarettes.

I recommend a slow, steady reduction in the number of cigarettes you smoke and in the amount of each cigarette that you smoke. In this program, you will gradually do this on your own as you understand more about yourself and your smoking. In the third section, you will make a concrete plan for quitting, if you have not already done so by that point.

I feel silly completing the exercises in this book. Can't I do just as well by reading over the material?

No. The material you contribute and the efforts at self-discovery you make are the most important parts of this program. The material I have written is merely a guide to help you discover the truth about your own life and your own smoking. Years from now, when you are on the brink of relapsing, you can review this book and your journal. When you do, you will learn that any two sentences you wrote mean more than all the pages I wrote. Your contributions to this book will always mean more than mine.

Anyway, which would you prefer? Feeling a little silly now, or dying prematurely?

I notice that I smoke when I get angry, and a cigarette helps me stay in control. I'm a little worried about what might happen when I quit.

I suspect that the people around you are a little concerned too. You have discovered that for you (as for many people), nicotine works just like alcohol, heroin, marijuana, or cocaine. It covers up feelings, delays the time when you will deal with your feelings, and helps you hide from your feelings. But the feelings don't go away; you just don't deal with them. When you are a nonsmoker, you will have an opportunity to deal with them. This may be a new experience for you, and as with all new experiences, you may not be very good at it. In Parts II and III, we will deal with how to handle these newfound emotions.

You mentioned anger as the feeling you cover up with smoking. Many people discover (after they have quit, usually) that they have been covering up feelings of hurt, guilt, fear, worry, embarrassment, grief, anxiety, inadequacy, boredom, hopelessness, and many other feelings by smoking. You may discover that anger is not the only emotion you have been hiding.

I don't like to talk about my personal life in front of others. Do I have to work this program with a group of other people?

No, you don't, although in my experience, the support of a group improves a smoker's chances for success. You can work on this material all by yourself and never share it with anyone. However, you will probably do better if you share your work with someone else.

You could work this program with your spouse, if he or she smokes. The smoking cessation literature uniformly shows that if your spouse continues to smoke after you have quit, your chances of staying quit drop like a stone. Or you could work on this program individually with a counselor, therapist, or minister.

If you're willing to share with people you already know, you could get together with a few friends, co-workers, or neighbors. If you would prefer people you haven't yet met, you could put together a support group of people who have never met before or who share a common interest (such as from church, a club, or a Twelve Step group). If you feel that a leader would be helpful to your group, you could ask a counselor or therapist to be your leader.

The experiences of people in group therapy, in Alcoholics Anonymous and other Twelve Step groups, in issue-oriented support groups, and in fraternal organizations all confirm that group support furthers their recovery and improves their success rate.

Give it a try. All you have to lose is your emphysema.

I'm a recovering alcoholic with six months' sobriety—this time. My sponsor told me not to make any major changes in my life in my first year of recovery. Quitting smoking would definitely be a big change. Maybe I should wait a while before I try to quit.

I am certain that when you quit drinking, your sponsor insisted that you quit using Valium, marijuana, and cocaine as well, even if you only used those chemicals occasionally or if you preferred others. Why? Since they are mind- and mood-altering, their use may trigger a relapse to alcohol (your drug of choice). Thus your ability to work a good program would be hindered by using any of those drugs. Nicotine is as powerful as any other addictive drug in suppressing feelings, and as long as you continue to smoke, you remain in the grip of an addictive chemical. You have bought into the propaganda of the cigarette companies—that smoking is an "adult custom," and that it does not affect your mind, your mood, or your health. If your sponsor suggested that you not quit now, my guess is that your sponsor still smokes.

After you have seen a few people with quality recovery die from lung cancer, become bedridden with emphysema, or suffer strokes, you will believe as I do—the time to quit is now.

As you may recall, Bill W., the cofounder of Alcoholics Anonymous, died from emphysema. Dr. Bob, the other cofounder, died of cancer. Both of them smoked heavily. You decide what makes the most sense.

I'm not convinced that I'm addicted to cigarettes.

Perhaps you're not. Perhaps you continue to smoke because you enjoy the taste, you like having something to do with your hands, or you like your image with a cigarette. Would you be better off if you didn't smoke? If you believe you should quit smoking because of problems you're having now or might have in the future, and you are not addicted, then quitting should be relatively easy. How easy has it been for you so far?

One value of accepting your addiction is that you will then understand that you cannot go back to smoking occasionally. If you already accept the need for total abstinence, there is no need to insist that you accept the addiction concept today. Keep it in mind, though—you may change your opinion someday.

I'm working this program with a group of friends. Everyone in my group has already quit except me. What's wrong with me?

Nothing. Remember that recovery is a journey, not a destination. The day you crush out your last cigarette is just one more station on that journey. Recovery continues long after your last smoke.

The real goal is to quit and stay quit. Anyone can quit; you "quit" every day for an hour, two hours, eight hours, or more. The goal is not to quit, but to *stay* quit.

Continue to work at your own pace, learning from the experiences of the others in the group. They are blazing trails you will soon be trekking, so pay attention.

Why are so many businesses and offices adopting smoke-free policies? It seems unfair to smokers.

It does seem unfair to those who want to smoke at work. However, there are more nonsmokers than smokers in most offices, and these people are often bothered by cigarette smoke. In a study quoted by Surgeon General C. Everett Koop in his 1986 report on involuntary smoking, 85 percent of people who had never smoked, 74 percent of people who had previously smoked, and 43 percent of *current* smokers indicated that smoke in the environment bothered them.

These businesses are trying to do the right thing for the greatest number of people. I know of only a few companies that insist that their employees do not smoke—most simply say that employees cannot smoke at work. Smoke-free workplaces have fewer fires and may pay lower fire insurance premiums than businesses that permit smoking; their custodial costs and furniture and carpet replacement costs are also lower. Smokers take more sick time and have higher health care costs than nonsmokers. Therefore, many businesses feel justified in trying to reduce their costs by favoring smoke-free workplaces.

Texas Instruments, a high-tech computer and scientific instrument company, now charges smokers higher insurance premiums than non-smokers, since the smokers have much higher health care costs. Other companies will probably do the same in the years to come.

Can the smoke from my cigarettes really harm other people?

The smoke from the mouth end of the cigarette is called "main-stream smoke." After the smoker is through with a puff, it becomes "secondhand smoke." Obviously, this smoke contains fewer pollutants and carcinogens than mainstream smoke, since it has already been filtered through the smoker. "Sidestream smoke" is the smoke from the burning end of the cigarette; it contains somewhat different pollutants and higher levels of carcinogens than secondhand smoke. Together, the secondhand smoke and the sidestream smoke are called "environmental smoke," and when someone who is a nonsmoker breathes this air, it is called "involuntary smoking." Public health authorities refer to it as "tobacco smoke pollution."

The 1986 surgeon general's report on involuntary smoking concluded that involuntary smoking causes illness and even death. Each year, thirty-five hundred lung cancer cases in the United States are attributed to involuntary smoking. In fact, the Environmental Protection Agency now estimates that fifty thousand Americans die annually because of it. The children of parents who smoke have far more respiratory illnesses than children of nonsmoking parents, and nonsmokers who live with smokers have measurable levels of nicotine in their systems.

Environmental smoke is obviously not as dangerous as mainstream smoke, but the evidence is clear that it is a cause of illness and even death.

What is the next part about?

In the next part, *Get Set . . .* , you will learn how you have come to rely on cigarettes to solve problems in your life and how you can handle those moments when you feel like smoking, and you will begin to make a plan for quitting.

The next section also contains some interesting vignettes and some inspiring stories of success. Why not open it today?

– PART II –

Get Set . . .

– 1 –

Goals of Part II

Congratulations on having come this far. By now you realize that this book demands a great deal from you. You will gain little if you just casually read through it. The progress you make will be proportional to the effort you invest.

Part II of *Quit and Stay Quit* will take you from accepting that you need to quit smoking to making a decision to quit. In it you will learn about the history and recent developments in nicotine dependence treatment. You will be asked to evaluate your progress and prepare for the next stage in this journey to happiness and improved health. You will have an opportunity to examine the roles cigarettes have played in your life. Before Part II ends, you will have learned many techniques to cope with the stress of quitting in preparation for proceeding to Part III.

When you began this program, your goals may have been vague. At this point, they are probably better focused. What are your goals today?

✎ *List your short- and long-term goals in your journal.*

This book will help you achieve your goals. You will discover that recovery from nicotine dependence will involve much more than just quitting smoking. Through the time and effort you invest in this program, you will discover a great deal about yourself.

Get set . . .

– 2 –

Stages of Change II

There is a well-known slogan in the Alcoholics Anonymous program: "Progress, not perfection." In the Quit and Stay Quit program, you are also striving for progress. Here is an opportunity to see how well you are doing.

✎ *In Part I, you evaluated your progress on a series of ladders to see how close you were to quitting. The same ladders and corresponding statements follow. After you have circled the **one** answer on each ladder that most closely applies to you, go back and see how you answered the same questions in Part I (pages 16–19)*

1. Contemplation Ladder

Please circle the *one* number on the ladder that most closely describes your thoughts and feelings about quitting smoking today.

10	I have decided to quit smoking.
9	
8	I am close to making a decision to quit smoking.
7	
6	I am thinking about quitting smoking, but I still have not made any
5	definite plans.
4	I am thinking about cutting down on my smoking, but I am not
3	thinking about quitting smoking.
2	I might have a problem with smoking, but I do not intend to cut
1	down or quit now.
0	I do not have a problem with smoking, and I do not intend to cut down or quit now.

2. Preparation Ladder

Please circle the *one* number on the ladder that most closely describes your thoughts and feelings about quitting smoking today.

10	I have decided to cut down on my smoking or to quit, and I have
9	already taken action.
8	I have decided to cut down on my smoking or to quit, and I expect
7	to take action within one week.
6	I have decided to cut down on my smoking or to quit, and I expect
5	to take action within one month.
4	I have decided to cut down on my smoking or to quit, and I expect
3	to take action within one year.
2	I have decided to cut down on my smoking or to quit—someday.
1	
0	I do not intend to cut down on my smoking or to quit.

3. Action Ladder

Please circle the *one* number on the ladder that most closely describes how actively you are working *today* on quitting smoking or preventing a relapse.

10 — I do something effective every day to cut down, quit, or prevent a relapse.

9

8 — I have done something effective today to cut down, quit, or prevent a relapse.

7

6 — I have done something effective within the last week to cut down, quit, or prevent a relapse.

5

4 — I have done something effective within the last month to cut down, quit, or prevent a relapse.

3

2 — I once took action to cut down, quit, or prevent a relapse, but I have not done so in more than one month.

1

0 — I have *never* taken any action to cut down, quit, or prevent a relapse.

4. Abstinence Ladder

Please circle the *one* number on the ladder that most accurately describes how much you are smoking right now or how long it has been since your last cigarette.

10 — I have not smoked in more than one year.

9

8 — I have not smoked in the last year.

7

6 — I have not smoked in the last thirty days.

5

4 — I have not smoked in the last seven days.

3

2 — I smoked less this week than I used to.

1

0 — I am smoking as much as or more than ever.

5. Maintenance Ladder

Please circle the *one* number on the ladder that most accurately describes the *longest* you have ever gone without smoking a cigarette since you became a regular smoker.

10	More than five years
9	
8	Two years
7	
6	Three months
5	
4	One week
3	
2	One day
1	
0	One hour

6. Relapse Ladder

Mark this ladder *only* if you did not smoke today.

Please circle the *one* number on the ladder that best describes how close you are to smoking again.

10	I no longer consider smoking again.
9	
8	I rarely consider smoking again.
7	
6	I occasionally consider smoking again.
5	
4	I frequently consider smoking again.
3	
2	I intend to smoke again.
1	
0	I have not yet started smoking again, but I have had a cigarette in my hand *within the last week* and almost smoked it.

Summary: Stages of Change Ladders

Record here the number you circled on each ladder. Go back to your scores on page 19 and fill in those numbers under the column for Part I below. Then fill in your scores for Part II (pages 80–82). The higher the numbers, the more progress you are making.

Date _____

	PART I	PART II
1. Contemplation *(Thinking about quitting)*	_____	_____
2. Preparation *(Making a decision to quit)*	_____	_____
3. Action *(Taking action to quit)*	_____	_____
4. Abstinence *(Staying quit now)*	_____	_____
5. Maintenance *(My experience of staying quit)*	_____	_____
6. Relapse *(Making sure I stay quit)*	_____	_____

You will be able to measure your progress when you complete a similar section in Part III.

History of Nicotine Dependence Treatment

The tobacco plant is native to the Western Hemisphere and was gathered and cultivated (mainly for ceremonial purposes) by the native people of the Americas long before the arrival of the Europeans. A Mayan stone carving believed to be from the seventh or eighth century shows tobacco being smoked. Christopher Columbus described seeing the Native Americans he met smoking tobacco. Sir Walter Raleigh brought tobacco from the Jamestown colony back to England and popularized its use.

Smoking has generated strong opinions ever since. George Washington encouraged its use; Benjamin Rush (the leading eighteenth-century American physician and today acknowledged as the father of American psychiatry) condemned tobacco use. Nineteenth-century physicians debated the risks and benefits of tobacco, although they didn't know what the chemicals in the leaf actually were and had no experimental evidence on the effects of smoking.

Scientific evidence about the dangers of smoking has been discovered relatively recently, but there has been social and moral pressure to quit smoking since tobacco first came to the attention of Europeans. This antismoking sentiment was based primarily on the discomfort of nonsmokers in smoky environments. Prior to the twentieth century, tobacco products were harsh and unblended; there were no packaged cigarettes, so people smoked pipes, cigars, and hand-rolled cigarettes. Chewing tobacco and dry snuff were as popular as smoked tobacco. As you might imagine, tobacco users made quite a mess, much more so than today. Their smoke was thick and acrid; smokeless tobacco users spit their juice into public containers or on the ground. Few women used tobacco; those who did, did so in private. Smoking and chewing became a rite of passage to adulthood for boys and a major social activity for men.

In 1913 the R. J. Reynolds Tobacco Company, which made smokeless tobacco and roll-your-own smoking tobacco, introduced the first machine-rolled and prepackaged cigarettes, Camel. The production and sale of tobacco products soared.

Mr. R. J. Reynolds used and enjoyed his company's products (especially chewing tobacco), but he was also a concerned public citizen. In 1913 smoking tobacco wasn't known to be harmful, but Mr. Reynolds feared that the paper he planned to use for Camels, which contained a flame retardant to keep it burning at the proper rate, might endanger the health of his customers. He held up the sale of Camels until his research scientists assured him that the paper was safe.

Ironically, his son, R. J. Reynolds Jr., died of emphysema from smoking Camels and Winstons, his company's major brands. Patrick Reynolds, grandson of R. J. and now a clean-air advocate, describes the company's colorful history and the consequences of tobacco use on his family in his book *The Gilded Leaf: Triumph, Tragedy, and Tobacco.*

Tobacco use really took off after Camels were introduced. Other brands followed, and many companies started making and selling cigarettes. At that time, medical science was in its infancy; most medical reports were anecdotal rather than experimental or investigative. There was no accepted, proven association between tobacco and any human illness until the 1950s.

By 1960, medical research had developed a significant body of evidence linking smoking to lung cancer. In 1962, Surgeon General Luther Terry appointed an advisory committee to report to him on the health risks of smoking. In 1964, this committee released its report over his signature, conclusively demonstrating that cigarette smoking was a cause of lung cancer and emphysema. Subsequent reports from Dr. Terry and his successors have gathered more data and reaffirmed and expanded the conclusions that tobacco not only causes several types of cancer, but also causes emphysema and contributes to heart disease and stroke.

On the strength of such evidence, many smokers decided to quit. About 90 percent of all smokers who have quit have done so completely on their own, with no assistance from therapists or physicians, and with little help from other smokers. Year by year, more people quit and fewer take up smoking, *except for teenage girls,* who are now starting to smoke at the same rate as teenage boys. In addition, more men than women are quitting smoking, so that within the next few years, there will probably be as many female smokers as male smokers.

Long before smoking cessation was a popular idea, the Seventh-Day Adventist churches and hospitals developed smoking cessation programs. In the 1980s the American Heart Association, the American Lung Association, the American Cancer Society, and the American Academy of Family Physicians all developed materials to help people quit smoking.

Each of these groups, as well as many others, developed pamphlets and other self-help materials that provided suggestions and advice. The Adventists and the Lung Association went further, developing group programs based on a cognitive-behavioral and educational approach to smoking cessation. They trained physicians, nurses, and others in their techniques and made their programs available at minimal cost. Their programs were based on accepted principles of behavior change, and while they may not have been spectacularly successful, they have a solid theoretical base and have helped many people quit smoking.

Many less credible forms of smoking cessation treatment have appeared. Hypnosis has been used in a number of ways: to teach smokers to relax, to improve their self-image, to help them associate cigarettes with something unpleasant, and to give them the "suggestion" that they would not want to smoke. Hypnosis is a technique, not a treatment; the treatment depends on what the hypnosis therapist does *after* the individual is in a trance. Simply being placed in a trance does not result in quitting smoking. Some hypnosis therapists are highly qualified professionals, while others are exploiting the public's curiosity about hypnosis for personal gain.

Acupuncture falls into the same category as hypnosis. It appears to reduce craving for cigarettes when done properly, although the data on long-term abstinence after acupuncture therapy are not yet in. Placing acupuncture needles in points as little as a quarter of an inch (5 mm) from the real acupuncture points has no effect at all; therefore, the experience and skill of the acupuncture therapist make all the difference between success and failure. Since few states have an approved course of training and licensure for acupuncturists, you may or may not find one who is qualified.

Aversion therapy for alcoholism treatment has been around since the 1930s; recently, it has been applied to cigarette-smoking cessation. In this method, the smoker sits in a small room filled with stale smoke and cigarette butts and smokes rapidly, up to the point of nausea. The smoker eventually associates the sight, smell, and taste of cigarettes with nausea. Some clinics have modified this technique to rapid puffing (without inhaling) paired with a mild electrical shock to avoid toxicity from so much smoke and nicotine. This method is still in use today, although its long-term success rate, even for carefully selected patients, is no better than more palatable techniques.

Other methods with even less documented effectiveness have been used. Injections of vitamins and procaine into the nose and ears were popularized in France in the 1970s and made their way across the Atlantic. Ear staples in acupuncture points have also been tried. Various medications designed to make cigarettes distasteful or to decrease craving appear from time to time. Most of these contain lobeline, a chemical that blocks some of nicotine's effects on the body. Unfortunately, lobeline doesn't block nicotine's effects on the brain and therefore has no effect on the desire to smoke.

The Food and Drug Administration approved nicotine gum in 1984 and the nicotine patch in 1991 as medications to help smokers quit smoking. Other forms of nicotine delivery are currently awaiting approval, including a nicotine inhaler and a nicotine nasal spray. These devices provide the user with pure nicotine (identical to the nicotine in a cigarette), without the other toxic chemicals in tobacco. The nicotine reduces the discomfort of nicotine withdrawal and may help smokers quit.

Dr. A. H. Glassman serendipitously discovered in 1984 that clonidine (trade name Catapres), a blood pressure medicine, decreased a smoker's "urge" to smoke. Many physicians now recommend clonidine, taken orally or through a sustained-release skin patch. Further research has been contradictory; some studies show that clonidine helps people quit and others do not.

The Twelve Steps of Alcoholics Anonymous have been applied to more than a hundred human ills, including addiction to cocaine, narcotics, and prescription drugs; eating disorders; depression and anxiety; compulsive behaviors such as gambling, sexuality, and spending; dysfunctional relationships; and many others. Nicotine dependence fits the original model of Twelve Step recovery much better than most of the other problems to which these steps have been applied. Smokers Anonymous started in California in the 1970s as a grassroots application of the AA principles to smoking, but it grew very slowly. Because of a legal conflict, the name was changed in 1989 to "Nicotine Anonymous." It emphasizes recovery from nicotine addiction through spiritual renewal according to the Alcoholics Anonymous model. You can get more information about Nicotine Anonymous by contacting the headquarters in San Francisco:

Nicotine Anonymous World Services
Box 591777
San Francisco, CA 94159-1777
Telephone (415) 750-0328

The information is free.

The book in your hands is based on a method of treatment developed by the author called Recovery-Oriented Nicotine Addiction Therapy. It incorporates the Twelve Step principles of Alcoholics Anonymous into a therapy method that relies on cognitive dissonance to produce a gradual reduction in the number of cigarettes the client smokes. The program materials include information, examples, and exercises that emphasize the discrepancy between what clients believe and what they do.

The most effective programs have been comprehensive ones that include education, information, and suggestions; medication to reduce craving; and an opportunity to look at the roles cigarettes have played in the clients' lives. Such programs take a "shotgun" approach; since no one knows what part will work for which client, all clients get everything. Many researchers around the world are now engaged in investigating means for better tailoring the treatment to the client.

Today, nicotine addiction treatment is about where alcohol addiction treatment was in 1939. Fly-by-night methods with no scientific validity come and go. Honest, qualified therapists and doctors do their best and often fail. Research continues, although with very poor funding. California has again led the way, increasing the tax on cigarettes and designating some of those funds for research. The next few years will probably see significant improvements in smoking cessation methods and nicotine dependence treatments. Perhaps you will contribute to them.

– 4 –

Cigarettes Are Your Best Friend

When people become dependent on a chemical, it becomes the focus of their lives. As their addiction becomes more intense, planning to obtain, obtaining, planning to use, and using the chemical occupy a greater and greater portion of their time. Eventually, they become completely obsessed with obtaining and using the chemical.

This is as true for cigarette addicts as it is for heroin addicts. Although it would appear that a heroin addict's life is considerably more disrupted than yours, *for you,* the disruption in *your* life is all that counts.

When smokers quit, they go through the same grieving process that people go through when they suffer a great loss, when a loved one dies, or when they move out of their hometown. You may have to endure this grief too. After all, you have become more attached to your cigarettes than you ever were to any of your friends. What friend did you ever see forty times a day? What friend have you eaten with, drunk with, laughed with, and cried with every single day? What friend have you taken to work, taken to dinner, and taken to the bathroom? You spend more time with your cigarettes than you do with your spouse, your kids, your parents, or your pet. Every phase of your life has been connected in some way with smoking. You turn to your cigarettes dozens of times each day.

And while you cannot always count on your friends (they have their own petty worries and priorities), you *can* always count on your cigarettes. They are consistent; they never change. They always look the same, taste the same, and make you feel the same. Cigarettes are truly your best friend.

Best friends share your interests and respect your opinions. They are always ready to lend a hand when you are in need. They understand and support you when you feel hurt or abused. They offer you quiet companionship and a shoulder to cry on. Perhaps you have been burned by "friends" who had their own agendas and left you holding the bag. But cigarettes have always been consistent and trustworthy. When you feel anxious, tense, or embarrassed, you can always count on the relief your cigarettes provide. Your next cigarette will be just as reliable as this one. Your next pack will be just as dependable as this one. This friend never varies.

But now you are beginning to realize that cigarettes have become a false friend.

You trusted them, and now they have turned against you. You relied on them, and now they are causing you pain. You defended them, and now they are slowly suffocating you. How could your friend do this to you after all these years together? And yet, the truth of this friend's deception is right under your nose.

This fact will not be easy to accept.

At first, you will want to make excuses for your cigarettes:

They didn't know what they were doing; it wasn't really their fault; please give them another chance.

But in the end, you will accept what they have done to you.

At first, you will deny the severity of what has happened to you:

My cough isn't really that bad; I can get along just fine if I just take my time; all I really need to do is to lose a few pounds.

But in the end, you will understand it.

At first, you will cling to the fantasy that everything will be all right:

I'll switch to a low-tar brand; maybe I'll quit for Lent; I hear that menthol is actually good for your lungs because it makes you breathe deeper.

But in the end, you will know that you can no longer live this delusion.

No wonder you are having so much trouble quitting! Giving up a good friend, even one who has harmed you, really hurts. And it will take time.

That pack of cigarettes is your best friend. A woman in a group working this program related that she had cut down to seven cigarettes a day and had stayed at that level for weeks—but could not cut down further. She was feeling so guilty and embarrassed that she didn't even want to show up for group meetings. She felt hopeless. *It's no good,* she remembered thinking. *I might as well give up.* She bought a carton of cigarettes and went back to smoking a pack a day. Later, she changed her mind and returned to the group, where she described what had happened to her.

Why, when nearing success, did she give up so easily? Why was she unable to drop below seven cigarettes a day?

For this woman, smoking was a reliable defense against the pain in her life. Sure, she had been gaining sobriety skills (just as you are), but she secretly felt that she was being unfair to her cigarettes—they had been so good to her for so long. And the idea of announcing that she was quitting for good was too much of a threat to her. So at the point when she was almost off cigarettes, she had to "run away."

Fortunately, she was able to resume her progress. And the other members of her group learned how difficult it can be to reject such an old, trusted friend. They learned to understand that an old friend can become a false friend. Once generous, a friend can become greedy; once reliable, a friend can become undependable. So it is with this old friend.

Giving up an old friend, even a false friend, is difficult for anyone. You may feel cheated, lied to, or foolishly naive. When evidence of your friend's hypocrisy becomes undeniable, you may pretend the two of you were never friends at all. This will not help. It is better to accept the truth of your prior friendship and the more painful truth of your abandonment by this old friend.

Your cigarettes *have* been good friends—there is no point in denying this. Accept it, and move on.

✎ *In what ways have cigarettes been a good friend to you? List them in your journal.*

- They helped me with . . .
- They comforted me when . . .
- They gave me something to do when . . .
- I turned to them when . . .
- They made me feel better about . . .
- They rescued me when I felt . . .
- They lifted me up when . . .
- They made me feel sophisticated when . . .
- They helped me break the ice at . . .
- I used them to appear older at . . .
- I used them to appear younger at . . .
- and . . .

Yes, cigarettes have been a very good, reliable friend to you over the years. But now, cigarettes are hurting you. They have become a false friend.

Here are some ways in which cigarettes have become a false friend:

- They roast my lungs.
- They sap my energy.
- They stink up my house—I am ashamed of my house because it smells so bad.
- They make my nonsmoking friends uncomfortable with me.
- They control my life.
- They gave my father emphysema.
- They gave my uncle heart disease.
- They make my clothes and hair smell like stale smoke.
- They make me feel weak and stupid.
- They cause me to fear the future.
- They have stolen my self-respect.
- They make me avoid places where smoking isn't allowed.
- When I crave a cigarette, I can't concentrate on anything else.
- My need to smoke has limited the types of jobs I look for.
- I waste at least an hour a day smoking.
- My family is very concerned about my health, but that hasn't stopped me from smoking.
- and . . .

These lists move you toward your goals, because by confronting the pain and losses that have resulted from your smoking, you will gain *freedom* from your smoking addiction.

A woman in another smoking cessation group told this story: "Once, I managed to cut down to half a dozen cigarettes a day and then

I just couldn't seem to cut down any more. It was during the Christmas holidays, and I was under a lot of stress: my husband had been ill, my family was coming to visit, money was tight, things weren't going well at work—one thing after another." She said that she felt as if she would explode. "Something had to give," she said, "so I decided it was better to go ahead and smoke."

She meant that she could not think of any other alternatives. It was either smoke or be splattered all over the room. But she *did* have alternatives. She knew what she *could* do, but she was unwilling or unable to choose those alternatives because quitting smoking meant *leaving her best friend,* and she was not yet ready.

So she smoked a cigarette. Immediately, she felt much better. Relieved. Calmer. She didn't explode, as she had been afraid she might. All for the price of a single cigarette—about ten cents. Look at the solace and relief she got for a few cents. And she could get more of that relief forty times a day for less than five dollars. Where else could she get so much satisfaction for so little? (And if she really did give them up, where would she turn for help?)

So for many smokers, the last hurdle to finally quitting smoking and staying quit is understanding that they will feel a loss when they leave their old reliable friend. It is *normal* to feel uncomfortable in doing so, but that is what you must do.

Did you ever have a boyfriend or a girlfriend that you *knew* you were going to have to give up someday—but you couldn't quite do it? Maybe on the *next* date. *I know,* you may have thought, *this relationship is not good for me, and one of these days we'll probably break up, but not quite yet.*

So it is with your smoking.

You know you need to quit, and that eventually *everyone* quits, and pretty soon you'll quit, but not just yet. Perhaps you have thought, *If I tell everyone I'm quitting, and I don't smoke all day, my God, that means I can't ever smoke again!* The immediate feeling is sheer terror. *What will I replace my cigarettes with?*

It is the same struggle alcoholics face when they face up to the need to quit drinking. Alcohol has been their best, most faithful friend. Other friends are great, but they have their moods, and you can't always count on them being there when you need them. But booze is consistent, reliable, and never asks for favors in return—and neither do cigarettes.

It is the same struggle bulimics face when they face up to the need to quit bingeing and purging. Bingeing and purging has been their best, most reliable protection from the pain in their lives. Other techniques are okay, as far as they go, but they cannot always be trusted when the chips are down. But bingeing and purging is available and predictable—just like cigarettes.

It is the same struggle cocaine addicts have when they face up to the need to quit using coke. Cocaine has been their steadiest, most consistent ally on the battlefield of life. Dealing with challenges as they come along sounds good on paper, but when addicts run out of energy and they absolutely must perform, nothing helps them handle the stress like cocaine—or a cigarette.

But when the lives of alcoholics are falling apart around them, when their livers are decaying, when they are about to lose another job because of unexplained absences—they have no choice but to quit drinking or die. They finally have to say good-bye to that good, trusted friend who has stuck with them all these years. Imagine the pain, the fear, the loneliness, the terror they feel when they realize they can no longer use alcohol (or cigarettes).

And when the lives of bulimics are falling apart around them, when their weight has dropped to seventy-six pounds, when their potassium is dangerously low, when they have collapsed again in an elevator on the way to the tenth floor—they have no choice but to quit bingeing and purging or die. They finally have to say good-bye to that consistent, reliable safety net which has been beneath them all these years. Imagine the emptiness, the isolation, the powerlessness they feel when they can no longer binge and purge (or smoke cigarettes).

And when the lives of cocaine addicts are falling apart around them, when their noses and lungs are so sore they can hardly breathe, when they have pawned everything they can get their hands on, when they have cheated friends and stolen from relatives, when they imagine enemies behind every door, listening in on every conversation—they have no choice but to quit using cocaine or die. They finally have to say good-bye to that magical, lyrical, energizing transfusion that has given them power and potency and has opened doors for them all these years. Imagine the confusion, the helplessness, the hopelessness they feel when they can no longer use cocaine (or cigarettes).

So what will be your choice and when will you make it? Will you wait until your lungs complain with every breath of air, until your heart rebels when you climb a flight of stairs, until you have burned holes in every garment and piece of furniture you own? Or will you realize that there is never a better time than right now to make that decision?

Will you hope for the day when there is less stress in your life, your problems are solved, your relationships are mended, your anxieties are conquered, your questions are answered—or will you accept that life will never be without stress?

Will you need to wait until finals are over, the Johnson contract is finished, the Joint Commission has completed its survey, Uncle Harry has had the operation, the kids have left for camp, the insurance claim is settled, the Dow Jones Average is up—or will you accept that now is as good a time as any?

It means abandoning your best, most faithful friend. Will you feel guilty leaving behind the ally who asked nothing and gave everything?

For many, cigarettes have gone beyond friendship and companionship. Eventually, they move in and become a lover. Smokers become attached to their cigarettes like desperate lovers, eyes blind to their faults, unwilling to listen to reason, resentful of interference by well-meaning friends, focused only on the relationship and its pleasures. Have you taken cigarettes as your lover?

This idea drew disagreement from some members of one smoking cessation group. But at the next session, one group member (who was a recovering alcoholic) told this story: "I didn't really believe that bit about cigarettes becoming like a lover until now. I went to an AA meeting last night, and the speaker was standing up there telling his story. He wasn't smoking, though it was clear he wanted to. The whole time he was talking—forty-five minutes—he held a cigarette in his hand, stroking it and caressing it. It was like he was making love to it. I saw then how cigarettes calm me down just by being near them, and how I get worried and nervous when I'm not near them."

For many, cigarettes become more like a member of the family. They share our joys and sorrows, they go everywhere we go, and they are with us when we have a family conference. They are with us at births, deaths, and every event in between. We would no more think of leaving cigarettes behind than we would think of leaving any other member of the family behind. Are your cigarettes like a member of your family?

One woman who was working with a therapist on quitting recalled that she and three friends (none of whom were smokers) went out fishing on a Sunday. Everything went well until she smoked the last cigarette in her current pack and realized that she had left the rest of her cigarettes in her car. The one she was smoking was her last one. "I insisted that they turn the boat around and drive back to the marina so I could get more," she said. "I couldn't sit still until I had a fresh pack in my hands. Then I was okay."

For some, cigarettes become extensions of their bodies. Maria Jacques, a therapist from Florida who works with addicted smokers, says that her clients feel as if they are being asked to cut off an arm when they face quitting cigarettes. You would have to be in extraordinary pain or danger to be willing to cut your arm off. Is it any wonder that addicted smokers don't want to even consider quitting?

One man told how he reached the point of being willing to quit. His sixteen-year-old daughter came to him, requesting permission to smoke at boarding school. Already feeling guilty about his own smoking, he become enraged. "You will *not* smoke at school," he shouted. He pointed at her, raising his voice further: "I will not have you . . ." and he stopped, looking at his hand. Between the fingers that pointed at her he held a burning cigarette. "At that moment," he said, "I came face to face with the insanity of my smoking." He turned away from his daughter, put out the cigarette, and turned back to her. "I don't want you to smoke," he said, "and I don't want to smoke either." That was the moment he made a commitment to quitting.

For that man, the cigarette was an extension of his hand. The cigarette felt familiar and comfortable between his fingers. When he pointed at his daughter, the cigarette was just another appendage, a part of his gesture.

Do you sometimes feel you could do without an arm or a finger better than you could do without your cigarettes?

You may not be ready, today, to leave behind this friend, this ally, this companion. You may be unwilling to abandon this confidante, this partner, this lover. You may be afraid of cutting off this part of your life. Anyone who has been through this will understand. This is not a decision to be taken lightly.

And yet, you have left behind other friends who slandered or exploited you. You may have separated from lovers who abused your trust or who found others they cared about more. You may have divorced your spouse when your marriage did not work out. You may even have severed ties with family members who were no longer good for you. So it should be with cigarettes.

If a part of your body were destroying you, you would need to remove it. Your cigarette, so helpful over the years, is now like a gangrenous leg, a once-healthy leg on which you used to run marathons. You may recall the past with tender nostalgia, but today's crisis requires major surgery.

For all that the cigarettes did for you in the past, be grateful. But for what they are doing to you today, you have a right to be angry. You can love them and hate them at the same time. Love and hate are not opposites; indifference is the opposite of both. You may never be indifferent toward cigarettes, but you may very well both love and hate them.

Getting something new often means getting rid of something old. To make room for your gleaming new sports car, you may have to sell your rusty old pickup truck. No matter how wonderful the new car is, you'll always think back lovingly to the old jalopy.

So what about your shiny new sobriety and your healthy new smoke-free lungs? They are gifts to be treasured—but recognize that you may grieve the loss of your cigarettes and your sooty old smoke-filled lungs. So even as you gain good health through quitting smoking, you may regret giving up the advantages of smoking.

What advantages?

Remember, if there were no advantages to smoking, you would have quit long ago. What were the advantages you got by smoking? To stay quit, you must counter each advantage with a disadvantage. Eventually, you will have to find similar satisfaction from something other than smoking.

Advantages of smoking	Disadvantages of smoking
I look sophisticated with a cigarette.	I could easily burn a hole in my new clothes.
My boss smokes, and I need to be as much like her as I can.	So when she gets emphysema, should I volunteer to get emphysema too?
When I get a little flustered, taking a puff gives me time to think.	When I can't figure out the answer and I try to cover up by smoking, everybody knows I'm stalling, and it looks worse than if I admitted it.
I really enjoy "taking five" for a cigarette break when I'm at work; besides, I deserve a little time for myself.	It's a lot easier to take a break than it is to work; I've been cheating my boss in order to smoke.

✎ *List other advantages and disadvantages in your journal.*

Cigarettes may look like nothing more than packages of nicotine, but they are much more than *just* packages of nicotine. They have advantages that smokers rarely recognize until years after they have quit smoking.

Think of all the roles your cigarette helps you perform. It helps you act out your dreams and live your fantasies. You can be sophisticated with a cigarette. You can be tough with a cigarette. You can be the center of attention with a cigarette. You can be self-assured with a cigarette.

Hollywood stars created some of their most famous roles using their cigars, pipes, and cigarettes. Joan Crawford, playing a New York socialite, waved a cigarette as she greeted her guests: "Dahling! So good of you to come!" Edward G. Robinson, playing a gangster, tossed away a cigar butt as he stepped out of a car. Humphrey Bogart, cigarette hanging from his lower lip, immediately became the center of attention when he walked into a room. And Clint Eastwood calmly lit his cheroot while half a dozen bad guys gathered in front of him.

Tobacco became a co-star for these performers, and for you as well. There are some roles that cannot be played without a cigar, a pipe, or a cigarette. Imagine the director telling George Burns: "Great show planned for tonight, George. But we're going to try it without the cigar." George Burns could not have done that show without his cigar; it was part of the performance. It was his co-star, almost as important to the success of the act as Gracie was.

Lauren Bacall, femme fatale, played her role with a floor-length gown, a cigarette holder, and a cigarette. Clint Eastwood, the High Plains Drifter, played his role with a sombrero, a poncho, and a cheroot. Edward G. Robinson, the gangster, played his role with a fedora, a snub-nosed revolver, and a cigar. Basil Rathbone, the sophisticated sleuth Sherlock Holmes, played his role with a cloak, a violin, and a large pipe. Walt Garrison, former Dallas Cowboy, plays his role with a cowboy hat, a Texas drawl, and a pinch of moist snuff between his cheek and gum.

What role do I play with a cigarette?

❑ sophisticated person ❑ salt of the earth

❑ tough guy/gal ❑ mature person

❑ independent type ❑ younger person

❑ comedian ❑ yuppie

❑ boss ❑ one of the in crowd

❑ cowboy ❑ wild and crazy guy/gal

❑ and _____

Is this really the person you are? If it is, you don't need a cigarette to be that person. If it isn't, will a cigarette make you become that person?

Some smokers become tense and anxious when they think about living the rest of their lives without this friend, this companion, this lover, this part of their body. Some smokers are afraid that they won't know how to handle certain situations. For some smokers, *anxiety* and *fear* are not strong enough words to describe how they feel.

How do I feel right now?

❏	angry	❏	disappointed
❏	resentful	❏	ashamed
❏	lonely	❏	abandoned
❏	guilty	❏	sorry for myself
❏	abused	❏	mistreated
❏	hurt	❏	inferior
❏	frightened	❏	frustrated
❏	embarrassed	❏	short-tempered
❏	depressed	❏	uncertain
❏	anxious	❏	inadequate
❏	hateful	❏	in love
❏	bored	❏	worried
❏	satisfied	❏	powerful
❏	relaxed	❏	out of control
❏	jealous	❏	exhausted
❏	grieving	❏	miserable
❏	negative	❏	paranoid
❏	withdrawn	❏	perplexed
❏	dejected	❏	desperate
❏	despairing	❏	mistrusted
❏	stagnant	❏	confused
❏	scared	❏	terrified
❏	reluctant	❏	concerned
❏	tense	❏	apprehensive

❏ and _____

These are all normal feelings. As you smoke less, you will discover feelings you did not know you had. With less nicotine in your system, these feelings become more accessible. Keep up the good work. The next few chapters will discuss feelings and will offer suggestions for dealing with them.

– 5 –

Getting in Touch with the Pain

Your smoking has given you lots of pleasure over the years. The cigarette advertisements remind you of it all the time:

- "Kent III taste—Experience it!"
- "Kent—Portraits of Pleasure."
- "Century 100's—Taste that delivers."
- "Vantage—The taste of success."
- "Heritage—Classic American taste."
- "Marlboro—Come to where the flavor is."
- "You get a lot to like with a Marlboro."
- "Merit—Enriched flavor."
- "Barclay—The pleasure is back."
- "Newport—Alive with pleasure."
- "Pleasure is where you find it. Discover Viceroy satisfaction."
- "Camel Lights—Smooth character."
- "Virginia Slims—You've come a long way, baby."

The cigarette companies are in the business of selling tobacco products, and they want to sell them to *you*. They decide on an image for their products and then buy advertisements designed to make this image appealing to smokers. They use words and phrases ("rich taste," "freshness," "pleasure," "satisfaction"), symbols (cowboys, wild horses, parties, spring days), and fantasies of youth and health. They want to convince you that cigarette smoking is desirable, enjoyable, sexy, healthy, and attractive. The nicotine, the smoke, the taste, and the aroma of tobacco give you pleasure, and knowing you are a "Benson & Hedges smoker" or a "Marlboro Man" is also part of the pleasure.

Tobacco companies put additives into their tobacco blends to make the smoke taste, and thus sell, better. They add flavoring agents (such as molasses, for sweetness) and chemicals to keep the cigarette burning at a steady rate. Part of the enjoyment of smoking is the taste, aftertaste, appearance, and feel of a cigarette. The cigarette companies carefully research and test their products for these factors. They want you to like as many things about their product as possible. They hope you will smoke long enough to become addicted so that you will smoke for the rest of your life.

Nicotine is the most important addictive chemical in cigarette smoke. It is a stimulant, with effects similar to those of amphetamines, cocaine, and other uppers. It makes the user feel more energetic and alert; it gives a real shot of courage and a brief respite from depression.

Acetaldehyde is also present in cigarette smoke. It is the first chemical the body produces from alcohol and has the sedating, addicting, and mood-elevating properties of alcohol. When you inhale cigarette smoke, the nicotine, acetaldehyde, and other chemicals in the smoke reach your brain within ten seconds of your first puff. You immediately experience enjoyable chemical effects, including stimulation, relaxation, and a decrease in withdrawal symptoms.

You also get considerable satisfaction from fiddling with the cigarette, the package, and the lighter or matches; in blowing the smoke out in various ways; in tapping the ash and rubbing out the butt. These actions help relieve boredom and anxiety by giving you something to do if you feel restless or out of place or if you need a little time to make a decision.

WHAT'S YOUR BRAND?

Each brand of cigarette is advertised as being made for a certain type of person. For instance, the Marlboro Man stands resolute, alone with his horse, against a backdrop of snow-covered mountains and blue sky—the picture of independence, self-reliance, and strength. Are you tired of being told what to do by people you consider inferior to you? Well, smoke Marlboros, and you can be as self-confident as this cowboy.

In 1988, the R. J. Reynolds Tobacco Company introduced a series of advertisements for Camel on the seventy-fifth anniversary of that cigarette's introduction. The ads boasted that Camel cigarettes were "still smokin'," and showed Old Joe, a cartoon camel, in various macho poses such as standing outside a Las Vegas casino, riding a motorcycle, and dragging a girl up the beach by her hair. The captions on the ads proclaimed that Joe was a "smooth character." Do you like to think of yourself as a smooth character, a macho guy who has a way with women? If so, then Camel must be your cigarette.

In contrast, Lucky Strike ran an advertisement showing an attractive young woman, casually dressed and seductive, wearing dark glasses and standing in a sensual pose, saying "Light my Lucky." Do you fantasize lighting her Lucky or having someone light yours? Well, smoke Luckies, and it's all yours.

Barclay cigarettes, sold in a distinctive black and gold packet, ran an ad showing a handsome, debonair man-about-town wearing a tuxedo at a classy nightclub, carrying the message "Barclay—unexpected pleasure." Would you like to appear more sophisticated? Well, then, you should smoke Barclay.

Virginia Slims goes beyond advertising in an attempt to be known as the cigarette for the liberated woman. Virginia Slims sponsors women's tennis matches as its way of telling women "You've come a long way, baby." Do you consider yourself a liberated woman? Then you must smoke Virginia Slims.

So choose your fantasy. If you want to be independent and confident, smoke Marlboros. If you want to be bold and masculine, smoke Camels. If you want to be sexy and feminine, smoke Luckies. If you want to be sophisticated and confident, smoke Barclays. If you want to be athletic and liberated, smoke Virginia Slims.

✎ *What brand have you smoked most recently? What image do you associate with a smoker of that brand?*

✎ *What brand did you smoke before that? What image do you associate with a smoker of that brand?*

The tobacco companies and their marketing experts know that you will choose a cigarette based on the image you want to cultivate. Each time you smoke a Marlboro or a Virginia Slims you confirm that image for yourself. Your choice of cigarette helps you feel more secure. And what greater pleasure can there be than feeling secure?

Through a psychological principle called *classical conditioning*, you associate the sight, smell, taste, appearance, and image of your cigarette with the psychological relief, the chemical "high," and the decrease in withdrawal symptoms provided by the nicotine in the cigarette. (Would a Camel smoker be satisfied with a Winston?) Eventually the sight and smell of your brand of tobacco will provide some satisfaction. (But would a Kool Filter Kings smoker be satisfied with a Newport?) And when you approach a cigarette vending machine with coins in hand, you will be irrevocably attracted to your particular brand. (Would a Marlboro smoker be satisfied with a Virginia Slims?)

You get so much pleasure from your smoking that you have continued to smoke in spite of all the problems it has caused. The pleasure is so great that you minimize the pain and deny its existence.

Everyone can understand the desire to escape pain, both physical and emotional. Everyone tries to avoid facing imperfections and failings. No one wants to suffer. *Smoking has* enabled *you to hide from your pain:* facing *your pain will help you quit.*

When you are smoking, the *pleasure* overwhelms the pain. The level of pleasure stays high for many years, even as the consequences of smoking increase. There is no point in trying to talk you out of your smoking pleasure. And as long as the pleasure exceeds the pain, you will keep on smoking. In order to quit and stay quit, the pain must exceed the pleasure. Since the pleasure of smoking is an inescapable reality, you will have to concentrate on your pain.

That means you will have to confront the tremendous damage smoking is doing in your life. Instead of denying the pain, you must face it. Instead of minimizing the consequences of your smoking, you must examine and accept them. Instead of making excuses for your behavior, you must acknowledge it. You are going to look your pain right in the eye, and when you truly recognize and understand the pain, it will exceed your pleasure, and you will be ready to quit. Intensifying your pain will help you win your freedom from smoking.

But the knowledge of the pain fades quickly, and the romance of smoking starts to return. That's when you must again confront the pain and bring it back to your mind. There will be many times in the future, after you have quit smoking for some time, when that "stinking thinking" will return, and you'll muse, *Hey, a cigarette sure would taste good right now; I bet one wouldn't hurt.* That's when you need to read this chapter again and once more recall the pain.

RECOGNIZING THE PLEASURE

What sort of satisfaction have you gotten from smoking?

- When I was tense, a cigarette calmed me down.
- When I was bored, smoking kept me occupied.
- When I was drowsy, a cigarette made me more alert.
- When I got embarrassed, I could smoke a cigarette and disappear into my own little world.
- When I needed to concentrate, a cigarette helped me.
- I just enjoyed smoking.

✎ *In your journal, describe the pleasure you have gotten from smoking.*

RECOGNIZING THE PHYSICAL PAIN

Cigarette smoking causes lung and other cancers, heart disease, stroke, and emphysema. In 1990 there were about 157,000 new lung cancer cases in the United States, 90 percent of which were caused by smoking. Heart disease killed 390,912 Americans in 1986; smoking contributed to the deaths of about half of them. During that same year, strokes killed 59,164 Americans and emphysema killed 47,058. In 1988 Surgeon General C. Everett Koop estimated that smoking causes the premature death of more than 300,000 Americans every year. The surgeon general now estimates that smoking causes over 400,000 deaths each year in the United States.

However, as you discovered long ago, the possibility of dying from smoking has relatively little effect on you. It may make you worry, but it has not made you quit. The physical pain you must recognize is not the pain at the end of life, it is the pain you feel *now*. Only *today's* pain will help you recover.

What sorts of physical problems are you having because of smoking?

- How does my head feel? How does it feel when I've smoked more heavily than usual? When I am craving a cigarette? When I smoke rather than eat? When I am in a closed room with lots of smokers?
- How does my stomach feel when I've smoked but not eaten? When I smoke a stale cigarette? When I'm nervous and smoke rapidly?
- Where are my burns? How many times have I burned my fingers and hands with a lighter, a match, or a cigarette? How many times have I dropped a lighted cigarette in my lap while driving?
- How do my fingers feel? Do my fingertips feel like pins and needles? Are my fingers becoming dull and senseless? cold and clammy?
- Where do I have tobacco stains? On my fingertips? On my fingernails? On my teeth or dentures?
- How does my mouth feel in the morning? Does my tongue feel like a moldy dishrag? Are my teeth coated with slime? Does it taste as though I've been licking an ashtray? Do oranges and tomatoes make my mouth and tongue sting? Does my tongue feel burnt? Do my gums bleed? Does the back of my throat feel raw and rough?
- How are my taste buds? Can I still distinguish subtle flavors? Do I have to load my food with salt or spices to taste anything? Can I still tell the difference between one fruit juice and another? one cheese and another? one cigarette and another?
- How does that morning cough make my lungs feel? What color is the sticky sputum I cough out of my lungs each morning? How does my stomach feel after I swallow it? How long do I keep coughing these days? Is there blood in my sputum? Have I had asthma attacks or bronchitis recently?
- Do I have constant problems with my sinuses?
- Am I having chest pains yet? palpitations? skipped heart beats?
- How are my eyes these days? Are they red and irritated most of the time? Are they bleary and watery? Itchy and dry? Does the smoke from other people's cigarettes bother me too?
- How is my endurance? Am I winded by a run up a flight of stairs? Do I get out of breath when I'm having sex? mowing the lawn? flying a kite? eating a sandwich?
- How is my singing voice? Is it what it used to be, or has it gotten gravelly? Can I still hold a note for twenty seconds, or do I need to stop for a breath? Does it now actually *hurt* when I sing loudly?

- Where in my body do I feel the craving for a cigarette? In my head? In my stomach? In my lungs? How much do I suffer when I can't get a cigarette when I need one?
- When do I crave a cigarette? First thing in the morning? Last thing in the evening? During a long meeting? In the middle of the night? Can I even go two hours without needing to smoke?

✎ *In your journal, describe the physical pain you experience as a result of smoking.*

RECOGNIZING THE EMOTIONAL PAIN

Greg Louganis, the Olympic diving champion, says that he used to smoke cigarettes. After a diving competition one day a youngster asked him for his autograph. As Louganis signed it, the boy said, "I'm going to smoke when I grow up too." Louganis was amazed to hear this and asked the boy why. "Because you smoke," he said, "and I want to be just like you." Louganis says that he decided to quit smoking at that moment because he knew he was a role model for thousands of young people and he did not want to encourage them to smoke.

Louganis was describing *emotional pain,* the discomfort people feel when they feel hurt, embarrassed, lonely, resentful, or disappointed. Everyone holds on to an image (often secretly) of the person he or she would like to be. Behaving in a way that conflicts with this image causes emotional pain.

What sorts of emotional pain are you having because of smoking?

- Am I really ashamed of the fact that I still smoke? Have I ever lied, even just a little, telling someone that I had quit (when I hadn't) or that I didn't smoke (when I did)?
- What is it like to be attached to a cigarette all the time? Do I feel as if I'm still sucking on a pacifier like a two-year-old?
- Have my repeated failures to quit smoking made me feel frustrated and unworthy?
- Am I frightened about the possible health consequences of my smoking—yet continue to smoke? How does that make me feel? Am I really seeking death? I know that if I continue to smoke as I have been, I am risking serious illness. Is there a part of me that really wants to get sick, or die?

- Have I lost self-respect because of my smoking? Do I try to avoid seeing myself smoke (in a mirror or in a photograph)?
- What do other people think of me when they see me smoking?
- Have I been inconsiderate of others because of my smoking? Is that the kind of person I really am?
- Am I setting the kind of example I should be setting for my children, my nieces or nephews, or other children I come into contact with? If just one of them becomes a smoker because of my example, how would I feel? Do I feel hypocritical telling them not to smoke but continuing to smoke myself?
- Has my smoking caused me to be embarrassed in public?
- Have I disappointed others because of my smoking?
- Do I sometimes feel foolish because I have to stop what I am doing to duck out for a cigarette?
- Am I sick and tired of having my life manipulated by cigarettes?

✎ *In your journal, describe the emotional pain you experience as a result of smoking.*

This chapter is about facing your pain, refusing to accept your old excuses, and becoming willing to accept a future without smoking. Getting in touch with your pain is not fun. But by intensifying the pain of your smoking until it exceeds your pleasure from smoking, you will come closer and closer to smoking your last cigarette.

At some point, you will finish your last cigarette and crush it out. You may do so with conviction:

That's the last cigarette I'll ever smoke.

You may do so with apprehension:

I just hope I can make it through the rest of the day without smoking.

You may do so absentmindedly:

Huh. I guess that was the last cigarette in this pack. Oh, well. I might as well quit.

Some people need to set a specific date to quit. They work best with lots of external structure. They pick a day in the future—the Great American Smoke-Out Day (the third Thursday in November), their birthday, New Year's Day, or an important anniversary—and work toward quitting on that day.

Some people smoke fewer and fewer cigarettes as the weeks pass, until they are smoking only two or three a day. "If I can get by with two," they say, "I can probably get by with none." And after a week or so of this, they quit.

Some people go through an emotional and spiritual crisis. They struggle and strive and get nowhere, and suddenly they break through and quit. This may be accompanied with shrieks and tears, or it may be done calmly, but it usually occurs abruptly.

Remember, though, that the moment you finish your last cigarette is but one point on your journey of recovery. *It is just another station, not the destination.* The most important work you will have to do comes *after* that last cigarette—facing the world without your friend, ally, lover, extra appendage, or co-star. That moment may occur today, tomorrow, next week, next month, or next year—exactly where and when on this journey it occurs is not particularly important.

This program is designed to help you quit and *stay* quit. So if you are having difficulty dealing with the idea of living without cigarettes, don't worry. Thousands of men and women are dealing with these same issues at this very moment. If you are working with a group, tell them about your concerns. This is a time for sharing, for giving and receiving support. Every person who ever quit smoking has to face the desire to smoke every day.

As time goes on, though, the intense desire to smoke will fade. It may never go away completely, but it does become manageable. A doctor attending a conference on nicotine dependence related that he had not smoked a cigarette in eighteen years, but that he had smoked a pipe for eight years after quitting cigarettes. One day, about six years after quitting all tobacco products, he was waiting in the checkout line at a grocery store and smelled the unmistakable aroma of pipe tobacco—his old favorite, Captain Black. The desire to smoke came over him like a warm wave. He searched around him until he found the pipe tobacco display, near the checkout counter. *How wonderful it smells,* he thought. *Maybe someday. . . .* But he chose not to smoke and left the store thinking,

What incredible power that tobacco has over me—no, what incredible power I let it have over me—what incredible power I give it. I have given tobacco the right to control my thinking. I now choose to take that control back.

This man was willing to recognize and accept his dependence on tobacco and to live with the emotional pain of understanding what he had allowed tobacco to do to his life. In his recovery, he became able to accept the past, to live in the present, and to look forward to the future.

When you work this program, you are not asked to attempt quitting until you are really ready to quit. Too often, you have quit when you were not yet ready or for reasons that were not your own. When smokers quit and then relapse, they suffer physically, emotionally, and spiritually. They feel like failures and become afraid of trying again. They have not failed, of course—they are just still working toward the day when they will quit once and for all. Each day is one more day on this journey of recovery. But the discouragement of quitting for a short time and then relapsing causes many smokers to abandon the journey. Take your time; continue working this program until it is clear that you are ready to quit.

Smoking your last cigarette is an important event, but *abstinence* from cigarettes is not the same thing as *recovery* from nicotine and smoking dependency. Putting out that last cigarette is one more sign that you are making progress, but it does not mean that your journey is over. In various reports, up to 90 percent of smokers who quit start smoking again within a year. If you want to be numbered among those who *stay* quit, you owe it to yourself to continue with this program beyond the day when you smoke your last cigarette. That day must be the one in which you make a commitment to continue working on your recovery.

The chapters ahead will help you get ready.

– 6 –

Understanding Your Emotions

As you reduce the amount of nicotine you put into your body each day, more and more of your suppressed emotions will surface. Nicotine, like alcohol, heroin, marijuana, and other addictive chemicals, affects the part of the brain that directs moods and emotions, called the *limbic system*. It is a relatively primitive part of the human brain and is under only limited control by the thinking part of the brain.

The result of chemicals acting on your limbic system is to change the way you *feel*. These chemicals alter feelings, substitute for feelings, control feelings, and blunt feelings. Most smokers are completely unaware that nicotine has these effects until they reduce their smoking or quit altogether. Then it becomes clear.

As you reduce your dependence on nicotine, you will discover (if you have not already) that you can use nicotine to mask anxiety, anger, embarrassment, fear, hurt, loneliness, grief, and a hundred other feelings. As you smoke less, you encounter more of these feelings. Some of them may be unfamiliar and some may be frightening. Some people give up their efforts to quit smoking when they experience the intensity of the feelings that emerge as they reduce their smoking.

Of all these feelings, anxiety is probably the most devastating.

Anxiety is the feeling of agitation and nervousness everyone experiences in stressful situations. The high school valedictorian waiting to speak, the Olympic athlete preparing to compete, and the third grader bringing home a report card all experience anxiety. Anxiety can be associated with hoped-for events as well as feared ones. Both the robber holding the gun and the robbery victim peering down the gun barrel experience anxiety.

Anxiety is with us all the time. We never succeed in eliminating it from our lives, but we do figure out ways of dealing with it. Cigarette smoking is one of the strategies you have used in the past.

If you've been a smoker for years and years, handling stress and tension without a cigarette may seem inconceivable. You have come to depend on smoking when you get nervous, and it really helps. You get a stimulating rush from the nicotine and an immediate reduction in withdrawal signs and symptoms. The nicotine improves your ability to cope with the situation. There is some evidence that the acetaldehyde in the tobacco smoke acts like a tranquilizer. One or more of the four thousand other chemicals in cigarette smoke may have an effect as well. You also have the satisfying physical activity of playing with the package, the lighter, and the cigarette.

You have found smoking to be such a successful treatment for anxiety, hostility, fear, and frustration that you seldom use the other techniques that are probably familiar to you.

If you are going to be successful in staying off cigarettes, you will need to develop other means of combating anxiety. You must become as adept with them as you are at lighting a cigarette. Now is the time to learn how to free your body from its anxiety and to release your body from its tension—and to do it in healthy ways.

Here are some of the methods people use to deal with anxiety:

- medication (tranquilizers)
- relaxation techniques (including biofeedback and hypnosis)
- increasing self-awareness (through psychotherapy, est, psychoanalysis, Alcoholics Anonymous or another Twelve Step group, Scientology, meditation, organized religion, and so on)
- behavioral techniques

MEDICATION FOR ANXIETY TREATMENT

Many people choose to deal with their anxiety by taking medication, and doctors frequently prescribe Valium, Librium, Xanax, Ativan, or related drugs. Unfortunately, these drugs produce a powerful dependence and outright addiction in many cases. You are already addicted to cigarettes—do you really need another addiction?

These medications reduce anxiety by throwing a chemical cloak over your mind. You are less anxious when you take them, but you are also less aware of what is going on around you and your mind is not as sharp. They make you less concerned about the consequences of your behavior (which is partially why you are no longer so anxious). Is this really what you want?

Some doctors give tranquilizers like these when they would rather not listen to your problems. Most doctors honestly want to help their patients, but very few have been taught counseling techniques, and many are unaware of the addictive effects of some of the chemicals they prescribe. In addition, most doctors are busy; it takes only twenty seconds to write a Valium prescription, but it takes at least twenty minutes not to. It would be better if more physicians studied addictions and recognized the potential dangers of these drugs, but ultimately, *you* need to take the responsibility for not getting hooked on sedatives, tranquilizers, or sleeping pills.

Taking medication is not the answer to anxiety.

RELAXATION FOR ANXIETY TREATMENT

Relaxation techniques teach you how to calm down your body's response to adrenaline and to control many of the functions we usually think of as automatic—like heart rate, blood pressure, itching, pain, salivation, and tension. You can learn to control many of these autonomic functions to a greater or lesser degree through these relaxation techniques, although it does take practice.

Basically, relaxation techniques, biofeedback, hypnosis, meditation, and T'ai Chi all have similar effects. Their goal is to put the mind into a state of intense concentration and the body into a state of relaxation. When you learn one or more of these techniques, you can channel your concentration and energy and learn to gain greater control over your body and your mind.

Some very simple relaxation techniques have much to offer you in the way of managing insomnia (the inability to fall asleep or stay asleep). With just a little bit of practice, you can learn to clear out your mind, relax your body, and fall asleep. These techniques will be especially helpful if you usually smoke a cigarette just before going to bed at night. When you master these skills, you will find them extremely helpful in your effort to quit smoking.

Through the use of relaxation techniques, you can learn how to handle everyday tensions more effectively. Everyone gets nervous from time to time, but for a smoker who is trying to become a nonsmoker, these molehills look like mountains. Ordinary stresses may set you up to start smoking again, but through the use of these simple techniques, you can gain greater control of your anxiety.

In fact, relaxation techniques can be so helpful that the next chapter is entirely devoted to them.

SELF-AWARENESS FOR ANXIETY TREATMENT

Many people seem to drift through their lives, never really understanding much about themselves. They never make the effort to find out who they really are or why they respond to the world the way they do. "The mass of men lead lives of quiet desperation," wrote Henry David Thoreau in *Walden* in 1854, and it remains true: most people suffer through lives constrained by their inadequacies, unable or unwilling to change.

A wide variety of therapies offer an alternative to this sort of life. They seek to give the individual greater insight, serenity, understanding, and knowledge of self. Improvement results from diligent application of the method. Many self-awareness methods are compatible with each other; for example, a person may go to church, be in psychotherapy, and attend Alcoholics Anonymous.

The Quit and Stay Quit program also relies on increasing self-awareness. Through the contributions you have made in this book, you have not only made progress toward living a smoke-free life, but also you have learned more about yourself.

In a self-awareness program, people treat their anxiety by understanding the thoughts, feelings, and beliefs that underlie the anxiety. Cognitive-behavioral and rational psychotherapies examine the effect of the anxiety and ask clients to accept the limitations that make them anxious. Insight psychotherapies search for underlying causes of anxiety and ask clients to give up their need to remain anxious. Spiritual programs advise seeking a "Higher Power" to help manage anxiety.

Any such program can help. You may become less tense as you discover answers to questions that used to baffle you. But there is a danger: you may give yourself over so completely to the program that you no longer retain free choice in other areas of your life. If that happens, the program has become a *cult*. No self-awareness program (including this one) has *all* the answers for *every* situation. You must maintain your own individuality.

The research on smoking cessation shows that you will need more than just an understanding of yourself and the answers to some cosmic questions in order to stay quit; you will also need some nuts-and-bolts methods of dealing with day-to-day anxiety.

You will have to look closely at everything in your life that makes you tense and check to see if you ever handle that tension by smoking. While you are discovering more about yourself, you must also search for concrete methods you can use to deal with anxiety directly.

BEHAVIORAL TECHNIQUES FOR ANXIETY TREATMENT

Up until now, smoking was your most reliable way of dealing with stress. You will no longer be satisfied with that way. Therefore, you will need to find effective, convenient techniques for dealing with anxiety as it arises so that you will not need to smoke. The rest of this chapter discusses active alternatives that may work for you.

An *active alternative* is a behavior, a thing to do, that focuses your attention and distracts a part of your body, thus reducing your anxiety. Since your goal is to avoid smoking when you get nervous, you will want to identify active alternatives that by their very nature preclude smoking. If you can find things that make smoking impossible (or at least cumbersome), you will have something to do *other* than smoke when you get tense.

You need to find things that fit in with *your* lifestyle and your character. You can't chew gum if you are a dental assistant or play solitaire if you are a compulsive gambler. In the pages that follow, you will find a collection of options and ideas; select the ones that make the most sense for you. Then use these ideas as a springboard for new and better ones for yourself.

People usually try to start with an *oral* alternative. Quite logically, they believe that since smoking is a very oral behavior, an oral alternative will be especially helpful. Oral alternatives, such as eating candy or peanuts when you feel like smoking, are particularly attractive to people who like candy and peanuts, but these alternatives may add inches to your waistline and fillings to your teeth. If you would rather keep your figure and your teeth, read on: there are many other choices.

Active alternatives do not have to be oral, but that's a good place to start. Which of these can you use today?

When I get nervous, I could . . .

❑ chew on a pencil
  – or a toothpick
  – or a plastic coffee stir-stick
  – or a plastic soda straw
  – or sugarless gum
❑ whistle a tune
❑ sing along with the radio
❑ click my tongue in time with the radio
❑ floss my teeth
❑ clean my teeth with a toothpick
❑ make a cup of tea or coffee

❑ or _____

Some authorities recommend avoiding sugar, chocolate, tea, and coffee while you are working on quitting smoking. If any of them trigger a desire to smoke, you should avoid them; if they do not, they are probably not a particular danger.

Sugar or chocolate may satisfy your need to chew or suck on something, but substituting high-calorie snacks for cigarettes can be devastating. If you put a bowl of M&M's or peanuts on your desk and eat a few every time you want a cigarette, you could end up eating an extra three thousand calories a day and gain thirty pounds in a month. The same goes for gum: if you chew gum occasionally, use any kind you like. However, if you chew a lot of gum, you should use sugarless.

Other active alternative behaviors work as well as or better than oral ones.

When I get nervous at home, I could . . .

- ❏ wash my hands
- ❏ dig in the garden
- ❏ water the plants
- ❏ wash the dishes
- ❏ brush my teeth
- ❏ do some needlepoint
- ❏ sew buttons and hems
- ❏ clean the place up

❏ or _____

Keep a list of ten-minute projects:

- ❏ Weatherstrip the back door.
- ❏ Reset the automatic timers.
- ❏ Remove the lint from the dryer vent.
- ❏ Glue that old chair leg back on again.
- ❏ Windex the TV screen.
- ❏ Alphabetize my albums, CDs, and tapes.
- ❏ Write a letter to the president.
- ❏ Play a computer game.
- ❏ Walk the dog.
- ❏ Clean the heads on the VCR.
- ❏ Spray for bugs.
- ❏ Do my nails.
- ❏ Spray WD-40 on my crescent wrenches.
- ❏ Check for lurking cobwebs.
- ❏ Collect all the change from my purse.
- ❏ Back up my hard disk.
- ❏ Watch ten minutes of the Weather Channel.
- ❏ Laugh at the pictures of my classmates in my old yearbook.
- ❏ Rearrange the clothes closet.
- ❏ Straighten up the pictures in the living room.

❑ Polish my shoes.
❑ Calculate how many seconds there are in an hour.
❑ Read the newspaper.

❑ or _____

Make sure you have a set of alternatives for the office too.

When I get nervous at the office, I could . . .

❑ drum on the desk with my fingers
❑ fiddle with a paperclip
❑ squeeze on a rubber racquetball
❑ walk to the front of the building and back again
❑ shoot baskets with wads of paper
❑ do some isometric exercises
❑ rub on my ring
❑ stretch a rubberband around my fingers
❑ rewrite my address book
❑ reset my watch
❑ sharpen my pencils
❑ make a list of memos to write
❑ untwist the telephone cord
❑ clean my glasses
❑ wear a rubberband on my wrist and snap it when I feel tense

❑ or _____

These actions could be helpful to you in a specific situation to counteract your anxiety. Please do not go on until you have added a few active alternatives of your own, ones that are specific and personal.

USING YOUR ACTIVE ALTERNATIVES

Now you can practice applying some of these active alternatives.

In Part I, you worked on a chapter called "Taking the First Step to Freedom from Smoking." In that chapter you identified the times you want a cigarette. Look back at that section now; reread it if necessary and complete the exercises if you did not do so before.

How many of the times you want a cigarette represent anxious moments? How many represent other strong emotions that you mask with a cigarette—emotions like anger, hate, fear, guilt, or sadness? Many situations that appear unremarkable on the surface have anxiety or other emotions underneath. Can you discover them?

For instance, take this one: *A time I really want a cigarette is when I am bored or have nothing to do.* At such a time, beneath your calm exterior, you might be feeling very tense because you feel insecure about your job or because you are making no progress on important projects. Alone with your thoughts, you may become worried about what awaits you at home or how your recent tests at the doctor's came out. Someone watching you sitting alone and smoking may see your boredom, but only you can recognize your anxiety.

Review each of the smoking triggers you read about and listed in the chapter "Taking the First Step to Freedom from Smoking." Which triggers are caused by anxiety? Which ones are based on using cigarettes to deal with other emotions?

Choose three triggers to smoking that are important to you and list them on a separate sheet of paper. Then identify one or more effective alternatives and list them next to the trigger, starting with "Instead of smoking, I could . . ." Here are a few examples:

Trigger	Alternative
I want a cigarette when I finish a meal.	Instead of smoking, I could get up and go brush my teeth.
I want a cigarette after having sex.	Instead of smoking, I could cover my partner with kisses.
I want a cigarette with my first cup of coffee in the morning.	For the next month, I will drink orange juice in the morning instead of coffee.

✎ *I want a cigarette . . .*   *Instead of smoking, I could . . .*

For each trigger to smoking, choose one, two, or three active alternatives that you could use. For the really powerful triggers, you might need a dozen active alternatives. An alternative that would work fine at home might be inappropriate in a restaurant, so find alternatives that are sensible in many different situations.

Just as you have discovered new triggers every day, you will also discover new alternatives every day. You can pick some up from other people who are working on quitting or from people who have already quit. The advantages of working this program with a group become clearer at a time like this. You may have a potent trigger to smoking for which you've been unable to find an alternative, but chances are, someone else in the group has experienced the same problem and just might have an answer.

Start putting your alternatives into action right away. Each morning, make a plan for the day, selecting one trigger you will resist. Choose three or four alternatives to have ready when that trigger appears.

Do whatever it takes to win the first round. Take it one day at a time, one hour at a time, even five minutes at a time if necessary. Each time the trigger appears and you don't smoke, take the time to give yourself a pat on the back for having done a good job. Accept some praise for doing now what you were unable to do in the past. Be proud of your successes, for from them will grow the greater success of staying quit.

CONSOLIDATING YOUR GAINS

When you find a powerful association with smoking and you conquer it—once, twice, three times, ten times—you are on your way to conquering it forever. As soon as you win a battle with a trigger, find a way to solidify your success. This is called *consolidating your gains.* Write a note to yourself describing your success in your journal. Each morning look at yourself in the mirror and say, "I'm worth the effort." Keep a glass jar on the counter; put a quarter in it for each success. Cut out a picture of something you want (like a new CD, a movie you'd like to see, or a new gadget) and tape it to the jar. Pretty soon you'll have enough money in the jar to buy it.

Consolidate your gains. A woman named Patricia who was in a smoking cessation group told how she could not resist the desire to light up a cigarette right at five o'clock. It was her reward for having made it through another day at the office (even though she rarely left before six). When she saw that the time was nearing five, her urge to smoke became overwhelming.

So Pat devised several alternatives. On Monday she left her desk at 4:58 and went to the ladies room. On Tuesday she transferred her phone to another desk just before five and worked at the other desk for half an hour. On Wednesday she took the clock off the wall a few minutes before five. Just a few minutes before five on Thursday, she slipped into an empty office and did five minutes of aerobics. On Friday at five to five, she told herself, *I'm much too busy to smoke right now . . . later maybe, but not now.*

Having conquered her "Five O'clock Cigarette" every day for a week, she wrote herself a note and put it on her desk: "Pat—Thank you for not smoking. Love, Pat." In doing so she was *consolidating her gains.*

Do whatever it takes, however silly it seems, to conquer the trigger. You will have then relearned healthier associations, and the urge to smoke in that situation will be greatly reduced.

Remember the college student who wanted a cigarette when she left class? When she became a nonsmoker, she became aware of the mess smokers make (like those cigarette butts outside the door). Whereas once this had been a trigger to smoke, it eventually became a source of embarrassment and guilt over her previous behavior. So she turned this problem into a solution: when she was tempted to smoke around the campus, she would look around for cigarette butts on the ground and tell herself softly, "I'm so proud of myself for not making a mess anymore." For her, it really worked.

As you put your alternatives into action, tell yourself that you are doing this to relieve the anxiety, to exhaust the tension, to defuse the stress. Tell yourself, "I am doing this, and I'm not going to smoke." At first, take it just one cigarette at a time—you don't have to stay quit forever, just for the next five minutes. If your active alternative can help you not smoke for five minutes, the trigger may pass. Success! Put many such small victories together and you will win your battle for smoking sobriety.

Which of your active alternatives are working? Which ones are duds? Keep looking for new alternatives and keep writing them down. Be creative! Be original! Be subtle. Be flamboyant! The more personal your active alternatives are, the more likely you are to use them, and the more effective they will be.

If you are working with a group, be sure to let the other members of the group share your victories and help you with your problems. It will help you and it will also help them. Your experiences will help guide someone who is not as far along as you are. Soon, you will be happily smiling as someone else relates a story of success.

These lists of triggers and alternatives will be important in your future. There will certainly come a time when your resistance to smoking is low and you will want a cigarette. The active alternatives you discover today may be your best friends tomorrow.

ANXIETY, ANGER, FEAR, AND PAIN

✎ *Are you now more aware of the feelings you control or avoid by using cigarettes? Which ones are you just now experiencing as you smoke less?*

I have used cigarettes when I felt . . .

❏ angry	❏ disappointed
❏ resentful	❏ ashamed
❏ lonely	❏ abandoned
❏ guilty	❏ sorry for myself
❏ abused	❏ mistreated
❏ hurt	❏ inferior
❏ frightened	❏ frustrated
❏ embarrassed	❏ short-tempered
❏ depressed	❏ uncertain
❏ anxious	❏ inadequate
❏ hateful	❏ in love
❏ bored	❏ worried
❏ satisfied	❏ powerful
❏ relaxed	❏ out of control
❏ jealous	❏ exhausted
❏ grieving	❏ miserable
❏ negative	❏ paranoid
❏ withdrawn	❏ perplexed
❏ dejected	❏ desperate
❏ despairing	❏ mistrusted

- ❏ stagnant
- ❏ scared
- ❏ reluctant
- ❏ tense

- ❏ confused
- ❏ terrified
- ❏ concerned
- ❏ apprehensive

❏ and _____

When you use cigarettes to manage feelings, you are using them in the same way that an alcoholic uses whiskey or a Valium addict uses pills. You are attempting to solve a personal problem with a chemical. If you do that, you might feel better for a while, but the chemical never solves the problem.

Personal insight helps a lot when you discover you are medicating feelings with cigarettes. Simply recognizing that you are doing it may be enough for some people. One man told this story: "My boss told me I had to work overtime. I had other things to do, but I didn't say anything. The next thing I knew, I was smoking a cigarette. I realize now that I felt abused, but instead of doing something about it, I stuffed the feelings by smoking. Pretty crazy, right? They were abusing me, so I turned right around and abused myself some more. Next time that happens, I'm going to recognize it and do something about it."

As you work on *dealing* with your feelings instead of hiding them behind a cloud of smoke, you may discover that you cannot handle the feelings that appear. Many smokers find that they need individual counseling to deal with these issues, just as many alcoholics find that they need individual counseling to deal with personal problems that they become aware of after they stop drinking. If this happens to you, please seek professional attention. Discuss your need for help with someone you trust. Bring it up in group (if you are in a group) or talk to your group facilitator. Ask your sponsor in Nicotine Anonymous for advice. Talk to someone who has been in counseling. Find a counselor or therapist who can help.

UNDERSTANDING YOUR EMOTIONS

In this chapter, you have looked at four different methods of dealing with the powerful emotions that drove you to use nicotine. Taking tranquilizers proves to be a poor choice. Relaxation techniques will help in certain situations. (The following chapter covers them in depth.) Self-awareness programs can help you learn more about yourself so you can deal with your feelings. And finding active alternatives will help you combat the urge to smoke when you get tense.

You will soon discover what works best for you. And eventually, smoking will no longer be one of your options.

– 7 –

Relaxation Techniques

In the last chapter you worked on a number of successful behavioral techniques for reducing stress. In this chapter you will learn another method of controlling tension within your body, called *muscle tension-relaxation*.

One part of the nervous system controls voluntary activities. If you want to hammer in a nail, you pick up a hammer, hold the nail in the right place, and swing the hammer. Your mind "knows" what you want to do, and it "tells" the proper muscles to do it by sending nerve impulses through specific pathways in the spinal cord and then through certain nerve fibers.

Another part of the nervous system is primarily involuntary. You never have to think about regulating your heartbeat, maintaining your blood pressure, or breathing while you sleep. A portion of your brain does it for you. These functions are called *autonomic,* which means the same as "automatic." Autonomic impulses come from the brain and travel through a different set of spinal cord pathways and nerve fibers than those that conduct the voluntary impulses.

The autonomic nervous system was once thought to be entirely out of conscious control, but today we are aware that we can affect it a great deal. With practice, skilled persons can control (within limits) their heartbeat, skin temperature, blood pressure, and level of tension.

In the first part of this chapter, you will learn to use muscle tension-relaxation exercises, one of the many techniques for achieving relaxation.

In the second part, you will have a chance to learn the technique called "guided imagery."

A number of audiotapes of exercises such as these are available through bookstores and mail-order catalogs. You may find them helpful. They are usually sold as "relaxation tapes" or "self-hypnosis tapes." Some have voice only; others also include music or relaxing sounds (like rushing water, crashing surf, or singing birds).

If you are working this program with a group, you may find it helpful to do some relaxation exercises together. Some group leaders are willing to let you record a relaxation session so you can listen to it again later.

Read through all these instructions carefully before beginning. After you get good at it, you won't need any help.

MUSCLE TENSION-RELAXATION

Sit in a comfortable chair, arms at your sides or in your lap, fingers loose, legs uncrossed. Loosen your clothing so you are comfortable.

Place your hands in your lap, thumbs up, and concentrate on your thumb. Examine the wrinkles of skin, the tiny hairs, the texture of your thumb. Look at the variations in color; look at the shadows; look at the light reflecting from your thumbnail. Concentrate on your thumb to the exclusion of everything else. Concentrate until your thumb is the only thing you see, all else fading into the background, becoming obscure and indistinct.

Breathe deeply and slowly. Become aware of each breath as it passes through your mouth and nose. Feel the air as it enters your lungs and then leaves. Breathe deeply into your abdomen, pause, and let the air out slowly. Concentrate on your breathing. With each deep breath that you take, feel yourself becoming more and more relaxed.

Concentrate on your thumbnail only. Concentrate on its texture, its color, the reflections you see; its shape, its contour, its patterns. All else becomes indistinct and unclear.

Breathe deeply, and relax. Allow your lids to become heavy. With each deep breath that you take, allow your lids to become a little bit heavier. Your eyelids flicker, and it becomes comfortable to let them close. Allow your eyelids to close.

Relax and breathe deeply. With each deep breath that you take, you become more and more relaxed.

1. Now concentrate on your index fingers and your thumbs. Pinch your right index finger and thumb together, and pinch your left index finger and thumb together, as if you were holding on to bits of string that someone was pulling. Squeeze as hard as you can for a count of ten:

$$1 - 2 - 3 - 4 - 5 - 6 - 7 - 8 - 9 - 10$$

Relax, and let your fingers and thumbs be loose and relaxed. Now repeat this, and as you do, be aware of the tension in your fingers and your hands:

$$1 - 2 - 3 - 4 - 5 - 6 - 7 - 8 - 9 - 10$$

Relax your fingers and your hands, becoming aware of the sense of relaxation and the feeling of calmness in your fingers and hands. Feel the blood flowing back into your hands, and feel the muscles relaxing.

Repeat these steps this time becoming aware of the tension in your fingers and thumbs, in your hands, and throughout your body:

$$1 - 2 - 3 - 4 - 5 - 6 - 7 - 8 - 9 - 10$$

Now relax your hands, becoming aware of the feeling of relaxation in your hands and throughout your body. Feel the calmness come over your hands and extend and expand through your body. Feel the muscles all over your body start to relax.

Breathe deeply, slowly, and relax. With each deep breath that you take, you become more and more relaxed. You feel the tension escaping from your body as you become more and more relaxed.

Now repeat this sequence using each of the remaining eighteen sets of muscles. To summarize:

- *Tighten the muscles to a count of ten.*
- *Relax the muscles.*
- *Tighten the muscles to a count of ten again.*
- *Relax the muscles, being aware of the feeling of relaxation in the muscles.*
- *Tighten the muscles to a count of ten.*
- *Relax the muscles, being aware of the feeling of relaxation throughout your body.*

2. Grasp the arms or the sides of the chair you are sitting in with your hands. Concentrate on your hands. Squeeze the chair tightly.

3. Put your hands on the arms of your chair or on the seat of your chair. Push down with your hands and arms. Try to push the chair into the floor.

4. Hold the arms of the chair with your hands, or grasp the chair's seat and pull up. Try to lift the chair into the air while you sit in it.

5. Hold the arms of the chair with each hand, or grasp the sides of the seat of the chair with each hand, and push together as if you were a nutcracker and the chair a walnut.

6. Clasp your hands behind your head. Push your head back into your hands as you pull your hands forward.

7. Place your hands on your forehead. Push your head forward and at the same time push against your forehead with your hands.

8. Put your right hand on the right side of your head and lean your head into your hand. Push to the right with your head and push back with your hand.

9. Repeat the previous exercise, using your left hand. Push your head to the left and push back with your hand.

10. Purse your lips as if you were holding a soda straw between them. Then squeeze your lips together as if someone were trying to pull the straw out and you won't let them.

11. Keep your hands comfortably at your sides, your eyes closed. Squeeze your eyelids shut as tightly as you can.

12. Take in half a lungful of air, close your mouth, and squeeze your abdomen tightly, as if you were getting ready for someone to punch you in the belly.

13. Now place both feet flat on the floor. Push down with both feet as if you were trying to keep the rug from being pulled out from under you.

14. Put your left heel on top of your right ankle. Pull in with your left leg and push out with your right leg.

15. Repeat the previous exercise, putting your right heel on top of your left ankle. Pull in with your right leg and push out with your left.

16. Stretch your legs out, heels resting on the floor. Touch your heels and toes together and squeeze your feet together.

17. Cross your feet in front of you, one ankle on the other heel, with your feet locked together. Now pull apart as hard as you can.

18. Put your hands in your lap, thumbs up. Interweave your fingers. Now squeeze in and compress your fingers; at the same time, pull out with your hands.

19. Put your palms together with your arms extended. Now push your hands together as hard as you can.

These exercises can be used whenever you feel the tension increasing in your body. When you become aware of anxiety, take a moment to breathe deeply and relax. Increase the tension somewhere in your body and then release it. Feel the tension decreasing. Eventually you will get very good at this exercise, and you will use these muscle tension-relaxation techniques very naturally.

USING GUIDED IMAGERY

Now you are ready to learn a technique called "guided imagery," which you can use to relax when you get tense and to fall asleep at night without sleeping pills.

With guided imagery, you first relax, much as you did for the muscle tension-relaxation exercises, and then concentrate on your breathing until you are deeply relaxed. Then your "guide" suggests a relaxing scene for you to imagine. When your mind is occupied by the relaxing scene, any tension-producing scene (such as the recollection of a conflict you had during the day) is forced out of your mind. As you become adept at guided imagery, you will learn to bring up the scene yourself.

Choose a scene that is calm and relaxing for you, that has few distractions, and that is part of your previous experience. Here are some ideas:

- You are standing on the beach, watching the waves.
- You are walking through a quiet forest.
- You are standing in a meadow, surrounded by wildflowers.
- You are a leaf, floating down a stream.
- You are a cloud, drifting in the sky.

Another imagery technique involves imagining yourself doing something very repetitive—something like "counting sheep." A good example is imagining yourself building a brick wall or the walls of a house, one brick after another and another and another. . . . Or stitching a garment, one stitch after another and another. . . . Or walking on a trail, or on the beach, one step after another and another. . . .

A number of commercial tapes that provide guided imagery exercises are available. If you are working with a group, you may want to do some guided imagery together and even record that session.

You can use guided imagery to relax when you are tense, to start the day off positively, and to imagine yourself not smoking in situations where you used to smoke. Many people learn to bring up a relaxing image quickly to counter anxiety, anger, or fear when it occurs during the day. You can also use guided imagery to relax during the day at times when you used to smoke and at bedtime to help you drift off to sleep.

Smokers frequently use cigarettes to deal with anxiety, frustration, and the irritations or annoyances of daily life. Guided imagery can be a healthier substitute. Using these techniques has made quite a difference for some people, and they can help you too.

– 8 –

Letter to Your Doctor

If you need a medical evaluation or if you want medication to help with nicotine withdrawal, you will need to see a doctor. On the following pages are two letters (one for men and one for women) that may help you tell your doctor what you are going through.

Just cut out or photocopy the appropriate letter and take it to your doctor.

FOR MEN . . .

Dear Doctor,

Your patient has joined a self-help program to help him quit smoking and maintain abstinence. I know you will applaud him for his efforts and will want to support this positive lifestyle change.

The program is entitled "Quit and Stay Quit," and it includes a series of educational readings, insight-oriented assignments, and behavior modification projects. I'm sure your patient will be glad to show you his book and share with you some of the work he has completed.

In the early phase of cigarette smoking cessation, nicotine withdrawal symptoms often become pronounced and are frequently the reason that patients are unwilling to stick with an abstinence-oriented program like this one. In selected cases, pharmacological treatment of the withdrawal may be helpful. Your patient may request such assistance.

Nicotine withdrawal symptoms can be alleviated by the use of nicotine polacrilex (Nicorette) or a nicotine transdermal patch (Habitrol, Nicoderm, ProStep, Nicotrol).

Nicorette is available as 2 mg or 4 mg pieces of gum in a unit-dose package; the nicotine is absorbed from the patient's mouth while he is chewing the gum and holding the saliva in his mouth. Some patients need as many as twenty-five pieces of Nicorette a day to relieve their withdrawal symptoms when they first stop smoking; since cases of dependence on the gum have been reported, it is wise to monitor the use of Nicorette.

Some patients do well with much less Nicorette; you may suggest that your patient try cutting a piece of gum in half and chewing it vigorously for a few minutes and then discarding it. This mimics the pattern of nicotine absorption from cigarettes and may relieve your patient's nicotine withdrawal symptoms while requiring only a small amount of Nicorette.

The nicotine patch is often better accepted than the gum. It is available in several strengths. Using the Fagerström Test of Nicotine Dependence can help you choose the proper size patch to start with.

Asking the questions will only require a few minutes. In our clinic, we start patients who score seven to ten on the Fagerström test on the 21 mg patch, and we start those who score four to six on the 14 mg patch. Those who score below four do well on the 7 mg patch, or none at all. At follow-up visits, we reduce the patch to the next smaller size until the patient is off the patch.

Nicotine replacement agents are helpful in the treatment of nicotine withdrawal symptoms, but not for the psychological aspects of nicotine dependence. They are not an appropriate treatment for depression, and smokers in whom such symptoms are prominent may do better on an antidepressant. In addition, they should be used with caution in patients with hypertension, congestive heart failure, ischemic heart disease, tachyarrhythmias, and the like. However, your patient is probably absorbing far more nicotine from his cigarettes than he will from the medication your prescribe, so the potential benefits of the gum or the patch most likely outweigh the potential risks.

Most patients complete their course of nicotine replacement therapy within three months. You should reevaluate any patient still requesting one of these agents after three months.

The other medication that has been found to be of value in cigarette withdrawal is clonidine (Catapres), which has been reported to reduce the craving for cigarettes and the signs of nicotine withdrawal in patients who are reducing their smoking. This potent alpha-adrenergic agonist is approved for treating hypertension; several good studies indicate that it effectively reduces some of the symptoms of opioid and alcohol withdrawal as well (although it is not approved by the FDA for this indication). The reasons for its effectiveness in treating withdrawal are unclear.

Although generally a safe medication, Catapres has known complications and potential untoward effects. For selected patients, however, it may be the best alternative. In a dosage of 0.1 mg twice or three times a day, Catapres may be helpful in reducing nicotine withdrawal symptoms and signs with little effect on the blood pressure. The Catapres patch has also been used with some success. In a patient with signs of autonomic hyperactivity or elevated blood pressure, Catapres may be the medication of choice. The usual conditions and warnings present in the package insert should, of course, be noted.

Beta blockers (Inderal, Tenormin, Lopressor, and so on) may also be of value in selected patients to block the excessive beta-adrenergic effects of nicotine withdrawal. I have no direct experience using these medications for this indication, however, and am therefore not prepared to suggest their use.

Sedative-hypnotics, such as diazepam (Valium), chlordiazepoxide (Librium), lorazepam (Ativan), and flurazepam (Dalmane), are sometimes offered to patients who are trying to quit smoking. I believe that the physicians who do so are well meaning and are responding to the perceived need of their patients for relief from the agitation and anxiety of nicotine withdrawal. In my opinion, however, these patients do much better in the long run to avoid the use of mind- and mood-altering medications, especially the benzodiazepines and the barbiturates. I have found that anxiety can be a strong motivator to work the recovery program aggressively and that the anxiety is not nearly as overwhelming as the patient expects. Many of these patients are at risk for other chemical dependencies; thus, the use of potentially dependency-producing agents is best avoided.

Let me turn for a moment to the medical evaluation you may wish to do.

Your patient probably wants to know the status of his health. In addition to your usual comprehensive evaluation, you may wish to include a chest X-ray, an EKG, and spirometry. Many patients feel better knowing that they have not irreversibly damaged their cardiopulmonary system. The discovery of a 20 to 40 percent reduction in FEV-1.0, FEF 25-75, or MVV may prove to be another helpful motivator; with addicted smokers, we need all the help we can get.

Thank you, Doctor, for your care of this patient. I hope that with your help, he will continue to work the "Quit and Stay Quit" program and that it will be successful for him.

I invite your comments and opinions. You may write to me at the Medical School.

Sincerely,
Terry A. Rustin, M.D.
University of Texas Medical School—Houston
Houston, Texas 77025

TR/rjr

FOR WOMEN . . .

Dear Doctor,

Your patient has joined a self-help program to help her quit smoking and maintain abstinence. I know you will applaud her for her efforts and will want to support this positive lifestyle change.

The program is entitled "Quit and Stay Quit," and it includes a series of educational readings, insight-oriented assignments, and behavior modification projects. I'm sure your patient will be glad to show you her book and share with you some of the work she has completed.

In the early phase of cigarette smoking cessation, nicotine withdrawal symptoms often become pronounced and are frequently the reason that patients are unwilling to stick with an abstinence-oriented program like this one. In selected cases, pharmacological treatment of the withdrawal may be helpful. Your patient may request such assistance.

Nicotine withdrawal symptoms can be alleviated by the use of nicotine polacrilex (Nicorette) or a nicotine transdermal patch (Habitrol, Nicoderm, ProStep, Nicotrol).

Nicorette is available as 2 mg or 4 mg pieces of gum in a unit-dose package; the nicotine is absorbed from the patient's mouth while she is chewing the gum and holding the saliva in her mouth. Some patients need as many as twenty-five pieces of Nicorette a day to relieve their withdrawal symptoms when they first stop smoking; since cases of dependence on the gum have been reported, it is wise to monitor the use of Nicorette.

Some patients do well with much less Nicorette; you may suggest that your patient try cutting a piece of gum in half and chewing it vigorously for a few minutes and then discarding it. This mimics the pattern of nicotine absorption from cigarettes and may relieve your patient's nicotine withdrawal symptoms while requiring only a small amount of Nicorette.

The nicotine patch is often better accepted than the gum. It is available in several strengths. Using the Fagerström Test of Nicotine Dependence can help you choose the proper size patch to start with.

Asking the questions will only require a few minutes. In our clinic, we start patients who score seven to ten on the Fagerström test on the 21 mg patch, and we start those who score four to six on the 14 mg patch. Those who score below four do well on the 7 mg patch, or none at all. At follow-up visits, we reduce the patch to the next smaller size until the patient is off the patch.

Nicotine replacement agents are helpful in the treatment of nicotine withdrawal symptoms, but not for the psychological aspects of nicotine dependence. They are not an appropriate treatment for depression, and smokers in whom such symptoms are prominent may do better on an antidepressant. In addition, they should be used with caution in patients with hypertension, congestive heart failure, ischemic heart disease, tachyarrhythmias, and the like. However, your patient is probably absorbing far more nicotine from her cigarettes than she will from the medication your prescribe, so the potential benefits of the gum or the patch most likely outweigh the potential risks.

Most patients complete their course of nicotine replacement therapy within three months. You should reevaluate any patient still requesting one of these agents after three months.

The other medication that has been found to be of value in cigarette withdrawal is clonidine (Catapres), which has been reported to reduce the craving for cigarettes and the signs of nicotine withdrawal in patients who are reducing their smoking. This potent alpha-adrenergic agonist is approved for treating hypertension; several good studies indicate that it effectively reduces some of the symptoms of opioid and alcohol withdrawal as well (although it is not approved by the FDA for this indication). The reasons for its effectiveness in treating withdrawal are unclear.

Although generally a safe medication, Catapres has known complications and potential untoward effects. For selected patients, however, it may be the best alternative. In a dosage of 0.1 mg twice or three times a day, Catapres may be helpful in reducing nicotine withdrawal symptoms and signs with little effect on the blood pressure. The Catapres patch has also been used with some success. In a patient with signs of autonomic hyperactivity or elevated blood pressure, Catapres may be the medication of choice. The usual conditions and warnings present in the package insert should, of course, be noted.

Beta blockers (Inderal, Tenormin, Lopressor, etc.) may also be of value in selected patients to block the excessive beta-adrenergic effects of nicotine withdrawal. I have no direct experience using these medications for this indication, however, and am therefore not prepared to suggest their use.

Sedative-hypnotics, such as diazepam (Valium), chlordiazepoxide (Librium), lorazepam (Ativan), and flurazepam (Dalmane), are sometimes offered to patients who are trying to quit smoking. I believe that the physicians who do so are well meaning and are responding to the perceived need of their patients for relief from the agitation and anxiety of nicotine withdrawal. In my opinion, however, these patients do much better in the long run to avoid the use of mind- and mood-altering medications, especially the benzodiazepines and the barbiturates. I have found that anxiety can be a strong motivator to work the recovery program aggressively and that the anxiety is not nearly as overwhelming as the patient expects. Many of these patients are at risk for other chemical dependencies; thus, the use of potentially dependency-producing agents is best avoided.

Women with premenstrual syndrome (PMS) may find their symptoms are exacerbated during smoking cessation. The use of nonsteroidal anti-inflammatory medications, such as naproxen (Naprosyn and Anaprox), tolmetin (Tolectin), ibuprofen (Motrin), and others, may be helpful. Oral contraceptives help some women. Other women obtain relief only with progesterone (not progestogen), usually administered as a vaginal suppository.

Let me turn for a moment to the medical evaluation you may wish to do.

Your patient probably wants to know the status of her health. In addition to your usual comprehensive evaluation, you may wish to include a chest X-ray, an EKG, and spirometry. Many patients feel better knowing that they have not irreversibly damaged their cardiopulmonary system. The discovery of a 20 to 40 percent reduction in

FEV-1.0, FEF 25-75, or MVV may prove to be another helpful motivator; with addicted smokers, we need all the help we can get.

The data on the increased risk of cardiovascular disease in women who both smoke and use oral contraceptives are incontrovertible; I would hesitate to prescribe oral contraceptives for a woman who continues to smoke. Babies born to mothers who smoke during pregnancy suffer intrauterine growth retardation and thus may have increased neonatal mortality and morbidity. Receiving this information may help a woman who wants to take oral contraceptives or who is pregnant develop the motivation necessary to quit smoking.

Thank you, Doctor, for your care of this patient. I hope that with your help, she will continue to work the "Quit and Stay Quit" program and that it will be successful for her.

I invite your comments and opinions. You may write to me at the Medical School.

Sincerely,
Terry A. Rustin, M.D.
University of Texas Medical School—Houston
Houston, Texas 77025

TR/rjr

9

Attitudes about Smoking II

Have your attitudes about cigarettes, smoking, smokers, and the future changed since you finished the first part in this series?

1. What is your attitude about cigarettes *today?* Here are some examples:

   - I'm ambivalent. Sure, smoking causes lots of problems, but if the government restricts the tobacco industry, there will be major consequences for North Carolina and Kentucky.
   - If some people want to kill themselves by smoking, that's their business. I have decided to quit.
   - Cigarettes are addicting. Why did I ever think they weren't?

✎ My attitude . . .

2. What is your attitude about smoking *today?* Here are some examples:

   - I didn't smoke today, but it's only because I didn't really have any choice. I still want to smoke.
   - Smoking is a disgusting habit and a compulsive addiction. Why anyone continues to smoke is beyond me.
   - I understand now that I became addicted to smoking. I don't hate it the way I did when I was a little kid, and I don't love it the way I did when I was in the service.

✎ My attitude . . .

3. What is your attitude about smokers *today?* Here are some examples:

- I still think smokers are pretty self-centered. However, non-smokers need to realize that people smoke because they are addicted to smoking and that they aren't trying to make life miserable for nonsmokers.
- I can see why people smoke for lots of different purposes. My reasons for smoking, and my need to smoke, might be different from someone else's.
- Most of them are probably addicted, like I am. That's why they can't quit.

✎ My attitude . . .

4. What is your attitude about the future *today?* Here are some examples:

- I'm doing all right. I expect to keep moving up.
- I feel pretty good about myself. I'm accomplishing some of my goals. I'm taking the future a day at a time.
- So far, I'm on track. I don't anticipate any significant problems.

✎ My attitude . . .

Part III also has an "attitudes" section. It will give you another opportunity to observe the changes in your attitudes toward cigarettes, smoking, smokers, and the future.

10

Questions and Answers II

I think I'm drinking more since I've been smoking less. Why?

Like other addictive drugs, nicotine suppresses feelings. As you smoke less, you have less nicotine in your system to keep your feelings suppressed. Many smokers find that they turn to other chemicals—though not always intentionally—to take the place of the nicotine. Some use Valium, Xanax, or other sedative medications; some use alcohol or marijuana; some may use cocaine or other street drugs. This will most likely happen if you have an underlying problem of depression or if you are addicted to another drug, like alcohol. A few years ago, when I was in private practice, I ran regular group sessions based on an earlier version of *Quit and Stay Quit*. I found that about 15 percent of smokers seeking treatment in those groups had another addiction. About 35 percent of all smokers are dependent on another drug, particularly alcohol. If you realize that you also have a problem with alcohol or other drugs, talk about it with your group leader (if you are in a group), a therapist, or your doctor.

I've been smoking less, even though I haven't been told to. Is this some kind of mind game?

Most people in this program find that with each project they work, they smoke fewer cigarettes. This happens because there is a conflict between what they are doing and what they think they should do. They resolve the conflict by smoking less. I'm glad to hear that you are doing the same thing.

You have probably noticed that some cigarettes are less important than others and that you can turn them down or delay them. Some cigarettes are inconvenient, and you may choose not to go out of your way to smoke them. You may now choose to skip one cigarette today—the one you smoke while walking the dog, or the one you smoke while driving home from work, or the one you smoke in the parking lot between the car and the office, or the one you smoke when you leave the health club. However it happens, you will be smoking fewer cigarettes each day.

This is very important in your journey of quitting and staying quit. Your body is becoming used to a lower level of nicotine. Your thinking mind is becoming used to handling situations without a cigarette. Your emotional mind is becoming used to dealing with feelings without smoking.

Because of this, when you reach the point on your journey when you crush out your last cigarette, you will not suffer all that much. The fear of the pain of quitting and the fear of the pain of withdrawal will turn out to be far greater than the pain itself. Quitting smoking from two packs a day is like jumping into the pool from the ten-meter platform—you will make quite a splash. But gradually reducing the amount you smoke each day is like hopping down the steps one or two at a time. Now when you dive in, it will be from the one-meter board, and you will make a much smaller splash.

By confronting your pain a little at a time, you have been taking away some of its power over you. Like a pressure cooker, you have been releasing some steam all along, so the pot is never in danger of exploding. Facing the pain of your addiction and accepting the past permit you to enter the future with a new set of choices. Isn't that what you want?

I decided to quit last week, so I quit. What's the big deal?

Congratulations! Although there are many people who have been able to quit smoking without much difficulty, they are definitely in the minority. Most smokers have great difficulty quitting and are prone to relapse. You can be grateful that you had no trouble quitting.

However, you are still at risk for relapse. Research studies document that within one year of quitting, up to 90 percent of people who quit smoking start again. Relapse rates among smokers are comparable to those of heroin and cocaine addicts. When smokers relapse, they seldom have a "brief relapse"; usually, they keep on smoking.

So you can be proud of yourself for having quit. Now is the time to really start working on recovery. With the nicotine out of your system, you will be more in touch with your feelings and you will be better able to work the important projects in this book.

My doctor says that if I don't quit smoking, I will get emphysema. It sounds bad, but what is it?

To understand emphysema, you must first understand how your lungs work.

When you breathe in, the air passes through hundreds of tiny tubes, called *bronchi,* into microscopic air sacs, called *alveoli.* You have millions of them in each lung. Blood runs in vessels through the walls of these air sacs, and the oxygen in the air passes into the blood. The carbon dioxide in the blood, which is a waste product of your body's metabolism, then passes into the air.

Emphysema is a disease in which the walls of many of the air sacs are destroyed. When this happens, the volume of blood coming in contact with air decreases; less oxygen is absorbed and less carbon dioxide is removed. The total volume of the lungs actually increases somewhat, but the *effective* lung volume decreases.

You wouldn't notice much at first. A little emphysema wouldn't interfere in your daily activities. You would only notice it if you stressed your heart and lungs, such as during exercise or when traveling to a high altitude (where each breath you take has less oxygen in it than at lower altitudes). If you continued to smoke and your emphysema progressed, you would become short of breath when climbing stairs, running for a bus, having sex, or lifting heavy objects.

Ultimately, people with severe emphysema cannot even walk across a room without becoming short of breath. You may have seen such people hauling around a small oxygen tank with them when they are out in public. A plastic tube carries oxygen from the tank to their nose; they must keep the tank with them at all times because their lungs cannot absorb enough oxygen from the air.

These people usually succumb to pneumonia because their lungs are unable to absorb enough oxygen when they get sick.

Emphysema is one part of the syndrome called "Chronic Obstructive Pulmonary (lung) Disease," or COPD. The other part is chronic bronchitis, the frequent episodes of mild lung infection associated with wheezing and the production of phlegm containing pus. These episodes usually respond to antibiotics and medications to open up the breathing passages, but they may progress to pneumonia.

Emphysema continues to progress until you quit smoking; then it stops progressing. Chronic bronchitis will get better within a month or so of quitting.

Of course, COPD is only one condition caused by smoking. Smoking also contributes to the development of heart disease, stroke, and cancer of many types (especially lung, head and neck, esophagus, and stomach).

The doctor said I have early emphysema. If I quit smoking now, will my lungs get better?

Yes. In the 1990 surgeon general's report on smoking, Dr. Antonia Novello concluded that most illnesses caused by smoking get better when the smoker quits. Depending on the disease, the health risk to smokers drops to that of the general population within two to seven years after quitting smoking. The chances are that after you quit smoking, your lung condition will improve.

The converse is also true: if you continue to smoke, your emphysema will progress. If you have early emphysema now, it will get worse every year you continue to smoke. When I was in the private practice of internal medicine, I saw many patients with severe emphysema. Every minute of every day, emphysema patients struggle to breathe; as the disease worsens, they must carry an oxygen tank with them wherever they go. They eventually cannot lie down and must sleep sitting up in a chair, and they cannot walk across a room without having to pause to catch their breath.

Bill Wilson, the cofounder of Alcoholics Anonymous, died in this way from emphysema. So do thousands of Americans every year. If you want to keep your name off that list, stop smoking now.

I really enjoy smoking. I'm hoping they'll come out with a safe cigarette so I can go back to smoking.

Tobacco industry researchers have been searching for a "safe" cigarette for years. R. J. Reynolds Sr., who founded the R. J. Reynolds Tobacco Company, was concerned that the paper wrapping his Camel cigarettes might release harmful chemicals when it burned and insisted that his scientists find a safe paper. Recently, the tobacco industry has introduced cigarette substitutes in an effort to find a "safe" cigarette:

- Favor, a plastic "cigarette" containing pure nicotine and no tobacco
- Premier, a high-tech device that heats nicotine beads with a piece of smoldering charcoal
- De-Nic, a nicotine-free cigarette

The failure of these products shows that smokers will not buy a cigarette unless it looks, feels, and tastes like a tobacco cigarette, and unless it contains nicotine.

There are many low-tar cigarettes on the market, but medical research has shown that these cigarettes cause just as much cancer and heart disease as regular cigarettes. Apparently, even the amount of tar in low-tar cigarettes exceeds the level of safety. In other words, falling off a 100-foot cliff does just as much damage as falling off a 500-foot cliff.

The tobacco companies will continue to experiment with alternative cigarettes, but they will never call them "safe" cigarettes, because that would imply that their other cigarettes are not safe.

What's going to happen to the economies of Kentucky and North Carolina if everyone stops smoking?

The tobacco-growing states have considerable influence in the House of Representatives and the Senate, and the tobacco industry has a powerful lobby in Washington. The tobacco companies have already diversified—into food products, beer, real estate, and a hundred other businesses. They have done quite well lately, and it will be years before enough smokers quit to affect them.

The farmers who grow tobacco will probably still be growing it fifty years from now. American flue-cured tobacco is highly prized around the world, and unfortunately, even after Americans stop smoking, the tobacco companies will find others to sell their products to. In time, agricultural scientists will find something else that will grow on the land that now supports tobacco plants, or other uses will be found for tobacco. (The tobacco leaf is actually quite high in protein, and animal feed can be made from it.)

Don't forget that the people of Kentucky and North Carolina have among the highest consumption of tobacco products per capita in the nation. They are suffering personally from their states' reliance on the tobacco industry.

Does making a New Year's resolution to quit help?

If it helps you, great. But make your resolution a reachable goal. If it is not attainable, you will abandon it. A resolution such as "I will work on my *Quit and Stay Quit* book each week" might be best.

I still haven't been able to quit smoking. Maybe I should take up smokeless tobacco—at least I won't get lung cancer from it.

It is true that smokeless tobacco does not cause cancer of the lung. However, it does cause cancer of the lip, tongue, mouth, and jaw.

Most people find smokeless tobacco disgusting. You might check with your friends and family before you consider it.

Finally, all tobacco contains nicotine. If you switch to smokeless tobacco, you will still be using nicotine. Everything that this book says about the nicotine absorbed from smoking also applies to the nicotine absorbed from chewing or dipping.

I already have lung cancer—from smoking, I'm sure. Is there even any point in my quitting now?

Definitely yes. Smoking reduces your ability to fight infections, and it causes bronchitis and emphysema. If you cannot fight infections or if you get bronchitis, you may succumb to pneumonia. If you develop emphysema, your lungs will have difficulty absorbing oxygen and getting rid of carbon dioxide. If you receive radiation therapy or have lung surgery, you will need all the lung capacity you have.

Smoking causes lip, mouth, esophageal, stomach, and other cancers, as well as lung cancer. You are receiving treatment for lung cancer, but this does not ensure that you won't get one of the others as well.

Smoking also contributes to heart disease, stroke, and arteriosclerosis. You could recover from lung cancer and still die from one of the other diseases associated with smoking.

Your chances of recovery from your lung cancer and of living free of other diseases will be enhanced when you quit smoking.

I'm a tax accountant, and this is my busy season. I was planning on quitting, but this seems like a dumb time to do it. What do you think?

When will there be a better time? You will be anxious and tense for a while after you quit smoking, but if you work this program on a daily basis, the symptoms will be mild and transient. As an accountant, you recognize the value of keeping track of progress and maintaining good records. I suggest you devote a few minutes of each day to working on the material in this book. Before long, you will find that you are smoking much less, and that the actual *quitting* will not be a monumental task.

I quit cocaine about six months ago and I'm doing fine. Now I want to quit smoking, but I'm having more trouble quitting smoking than I did quitting cocaine.

This is quite common. In a study by Dr. Jack Henningfield, experienced drug users could not tell the difference between injections of cocaine, amphetamine, and nicotine. These drugs all have similar effects on the brain and body. Therefore, if you have been using both nicotine and cocaine and you stop using cocaine, your body will want the nicotine even more. In 1991, I demonstrated this in a research study that looked at cocaine and nicotine craving in a group of hospitalized cocaine addicts who smoked cigarettes. When they stopped cocaine, they wanted their cigarettes even more.

In addition, smoking is probably a more powerful dependence than cocaine because there is more you can *do* with a cigarette and there are more places you can do it.

Finally, many recovering alcoholics and addicts get very little support for quitting smoking from their most important role models, their sponsors and supporters in Twelve Step recovery programs. The majority of these people still smoke and are reluctant to face their nicotine dependence.

Your problem is a common one. I suggest finding a nonsmoking sponsor, nonsmoking supporters, and nonsmoking meetings. Keep progressing in this book and discuss your growth with your sponsor. Add nicotine to your First Step and include your smoking behaviors in your Fourth and Fifth Steps.

I tried Nicorette; it tasted awful. Then I tried the patch, and it gave me a rash. What do I do now?

Many people dislike the peppery taste of Nicorette. Unfortunately, most flavorful gum is acidic, which prevents the nicotine in Nicorette from being absorbed.

One-third or more of people who use the patch have some skin reaction, from redness and itching to hives. Since there are four brands of the patch available, and their nicotine delivery mechanisms are different, you could try one of the other brands. And depending on the kind of rash you had, your doctor might suggest a cream to use along with the patch.

Catapres (clonidine) is a medication for treating high blood pressure that has shown some value in reducing the symptoms of nicotine withdrawal; your doctor might suggest trying Catapres.

Some smokers have benefited from acupuncture treatment to reduce the symptoms of nicotine withdrawal. Others have used biofeedback.

If none of these alternatives work for you, you can still quit smoking. This program advocates a gradual reduction in your smoking as you work your way through it. So you may not need nicotine replacement at all.

I'm having a terrible time quitting. I dropped below a pack a day, but I became so anxious that I had to smoke more. I gained ten pounds just like that, and I was on everyone's case all the time. I think my marriage was in jeopardy. Am I unusual, or do other smokers have this much trouble too?

Smokers who try to quit too quickly often have the same problems you describe. I recommend a gradual reduction in smoking—a reduction in both the number of cigarettes you smoke and the amount of tobacco you smoke from each cigarette. When you work the Quit and

Stay Quit program, this is what usually happens. It may take some time, but you can succeed if you keep at it. My father always told me, "Slow and steady wins the race." Slow, steady reduction in your smoking will win this race too.

Your symptoms are those of nicotine withdrawal—anxiety, weight gain, and irritability. Nicotine replacement therapy, in the form of the nicotine gum or a nicotine patch, may help you. (See the chapter "Medications for Treating Withdrawal from Nicotine.")

Part of your difficulty may be that you are responding to external pressures to quit—are you in a competition with someone, did you give yourself a deadline, or are you shooting for a reward for quitting? I advise against comparing your smoking dependence with anyone else's. The intensity of nicotine dependence can vary between individuals. You only need to compare yourself with your *potential*. It may take you longer than you would like to quit, but you can be just as successful as anyone else. Think of quitting smoking as a long sea journey—the sea looks the same to you each morning, but the captain knows you are getting closer and closer to port every day. It's hard to be patient when you have finally decided to quit, especially now that you have accepted the importance of quitting. The writer Georges Louis de Buffon once said, "Genius is nothing but a greater aptitude for patience." Easy does it; you are doing this for yourself, not for anyone else. Do it at your own pace, and after you have quit, you'll feel like a genius.

I've been told that cigarettes cause much more death and disease than marijuana. I like to smoke pot from time to time. Do you think that would be a problem?

Dr. Richard Schwartz, an expert on marijuana, says that one marijuana cigarette has the lung damage potential of five to ten tobacco cigarettes. To date, no cases of lung cancer can be attributed to marijuana, but there are very few people who regularly smoke marijuana but not tobacco. The lung cancer they get would be attributed to the tobacco, not the marijuana. However, the damage from smoking marijuana probably adds to the damage caused by smoking tobacco.

There is another problem in your story: the tetrahydrocannabinol (THC) in marijuana smoke is addicting. You are already addicted to nicotine. You need fewer addictions, not more. I advise you to consider marijuana as harmful as tobacco.

I finished Part I and I'm smoking only eight cigarettes a day. That's down from two packs a day for thirty years. I'm satisfied right now, and I really don't want to go any further just yet.

That's fine. You may need to stay at this plateau for some time before you are ready to move on. Many smokers, particularly those who are highly addicted to nicotine and those who use cigarettes as a tool to cope with stress in their everyday lives, need weeks or months to grieve the loss of their "old friend." You may be one of these people. What's important is that when you do quit, you stay quit.

There is a direct relationship between how much you smoke and the damage done by smoking. Smoking as few as five cigarettes a day has been shown to increase the risk of heart disease and cancer. As few as six cigarettes a day can provide enough nicotine to keep you addicted. So you will eventually want to reduce your smoking further.

It is also possible that you are smoking more than you realize. Research shows that some smokers extract nearly as much nicotine from eight cigarettes as others customarily get from a whole pack. They do this by smoking *more* of the cigarette, taking more puffs from each cigarette, and holding the smoke in their lungs longer (as marijuana smokers do). So you may be getting quite a bit of nicotine out of those eight cigarettes. Studies by Dr. A. K. Armitage showed that a smoker could extract as little as 29 percent and as much as 92 percent of the nicotine in a cigarette, depending on how it was smoked. So "cutting down" means smoking *less*, not just smoking *fewer cigarettes*.

Now would be a good time to notice how much of each of those eight cigarettes you actually smoke. You might try drawing a line around the cigarette and deciding not to smoke it past that line. Because some of the chemicals cool and condense onto the tobacco as they progress up the cigarette and become vaporized again when the heat reaches them, the final third of the cigarette actually contains as much cancer-causing material as the first two thirds. Cutting out the last third of the cigarette would be to your advantage.

I sometimes read a memo or a report and then realize I don't remember any of it. This has happened to me when reading just about anything—the newspaper, a novel, even this book. Sometimes I can't seem to retain anything. What's the matter with me?

There is nothing the matter with you. As you reduce your smoking and your nicotine intake, your brain has less nicotine available to it. Being used to running on nicotine, your brain will temporarily have difficulty with some of its functions. Keeping calm is one; being patient is another. Thinking quickly, retaining information, and making decisions are *cognitive* functions that your brain will have problems with at first.

These functions improve gradually. Some studies show that certain functions recover in a week; others may require many weeks to return to normal. In the meantime, you will have to make an effort to concentrate more, take notes, make lists, and take nothing for granted.

I am very upset with you. I did what you said and got into a group for quitting smoking. The next thing I knew, I was crying and spilling my guts out in front of a bunch of people I didn't even know. I think I was hoodwinked into that and I don't appreciate it one bit.

I am sorry you feel that I deceived you. I have tried to make it clear in this book that successfully quitting smoking and staying quit requires that you examine the roles that cigarettes play in your life. This may involve more self-examination than you have ever done before. For people who have never been in therapy or in a self-help group, this process of getting to know yourself can be extremely stressful. I know it was for me.

However, it is through this sort of self-examination that you will discover the truth about your own life. I cannot guarantee that you will be happier for having done it, but I believe you will be.

Perhaps you need to take a break from the group. Discuss this possibility with your group. Tell them you are feeling overwhelmed right now. Ask for their support. Let them know how stressful the group has been. I predict that the group will support you, and you may discover that you have come to value the group more than you thought.

I liked the idea of the relaxation techniques, but I wasn't any good at it. What can I do?

If you keep practicing these techniques, you will certainly improve. Purchase a relaxation tape at a bookstore or find a therapist who does biofeedback. If relaxation techniques appeal to you, they may be of great benefit to you in your recovery.

How can I find out how badly I've hurt myself because of smoking?

Your doctor can run some tests on your lungs called *pulmonary function tests*. In these tests, you breathe into a machine according to the instructions of a technologist. The machine measures the capacity of your lungs, how fast you can blow the air out, how much air your lungs can move in a minute, and other values. The function of your small airways (the ones most damaged by smoking) can then be calculated.

Damage to your heart is harder to measure. If you have had chest pains, your doctor may order an exercise stress test, in which you walk on a treadmill or ride a stationary bicycle to make your heart work harder. Meanwhile, a machine indicates the condition of your heart while a doctor and a technologist watch the monitors. If an abnormality appears, the doctor stops the test. In that case, the doctor might recommend further tests. If the stress test is negative, it means you have no measurable damage to your heart.

Searching for cancer is even harder. An X-ray of your lungs will usually show a cancer if it is bigger than one centimeter in diameter, about the size of the filter of a cigarette. However, cancers probably start from a single abnormal cell, so most cancers contain several million cells before they are visible on X-rays. Even if you have a normal chest X-ray today, there is no guarantee that you have escaped lung cancer. However, each year you remain abstinent improves your chances of never having cancer.

A friend of mine says she would think about quitting if I helped her. Would that be a good idea at this stage?

It would be a good idea to help *each other*. Avoid putting yourself in the position of therapist right now—even if you are not smoking, you are at great risk of relapse. Taking on the responsibility of someone else's recovery is highly stressful and should not be undertaken until you have successfully maintained abstinence for a couple of years.

This should not prevent the two of you from working together as peers. You can support each other in Nicotine Anonymous, work together formally on the material in this book, call each other daily to check on each other's progress, and provide motivation and encouragement for one another.

After you have each smoked your last cigarette, you can continue to be a source of support for each other. You will each face hundreds of situations in which you will be at risk for relapse. Those are times when you can call your "buddy" for support and suggestions.

I compared a recent picture of myself with one that's about five years old, and I was struck by how lined my face looks. Are those facial lines the result of smoking? Will they go away if I quit?

There is research evidence to show that smoking causes wrinkles and that they tend to go away after quitting. The wrinkles may be caused by nicotine's effects on your nutrition, by the increase in metabolism triggered by nicotine, by the drying effect of the smoke, or by some cause no one has yet thought of. Dr. Virginia Ernster and Dr. Deborah Grady of the University of California at San Francisco are currently running a large project to study this problem.

Is it harder for black people or white people to quit smoking?

There is no evidence that any ethnic group has more difficulty quitting than any other. The same goes for cultural groups, age groups, or gender groups. However, the rate of smoking varies considerably between ethnic and gender groups. In the United States, black men have the highest rate of smoking, white men are next, and black and white women have about the same smoking rates. Unfortunately, black men are also more prone to some of the diseases caused by smoking, especially heart disease. Education also plays a role: high school dropouts smoke at twice the rate of college graduates.

As adults quit smoking or die, they are replaced as customers of the cigarette companies by teenagers who start smoking. *Primary prevention* efforts to keep children from starting to smoke have been modestly successful; fewer boys are now starting than ten years ago. However, more teenage girls are starting to smoke than ever before; if this trend continues, there will soon be as many women smoking as men.

What is the next part about?

In Part III you will learn about the history of addiction treatment and the tradition from which this method of treating nicotine dependence evolved. You will review your progress to this point and set a day to smoke your last cigarette (if you have not already done so). Most important, you will develop a strategy to prevent relapsing and will make plans for continuing your progress into the future.

Why not get started today?

– PART III –

Go! . . .

– 1 –

Goals of Part III

You have now made a decision to quit smoking. This book will guide you as you finish your last pack and enter recovery. The first two parts demanded a great deal of you; this one will also. As before, the value you derive from it will be equal to the effort you invest in it.

In Part III, you will again set goals for the future and evaluate your progress. You will learn how smoking cessation treatment evolved from experience gained through the treatment of alcoholism and drug dependency. Using these methods, you will learn how to reduce your smoking to a very low level and will then set a date to quit altogether.

After finishing your last pack, you will have an opportunity to explore some issues in your life that will help you in your recovery. You will develop a plan to prevent relapsing and will review the progress you have made. Finally, you will look to the future and make plans for continued success.

Learning to set goals and pursue them is a valuable skill. You have already shown that you can set goals. What are your goals today?

✎ *In your journal, list your short- and long-term goals.*

This book will help you achieve your goals. You can be proud of yourself for the progress you have already made. Don't stop now—success is just ahead.

Go!

– 2 –

Stages of Change III

You have shown a high level of motivation to quit smoking by completing Parts I and II in this series. Now you will see how this change can be measured.

✎ *In the next several pages, you will find the same ladders you found in Parts I and II. Circle the **one** best response on each ladder, and then compare your responses with the ones you gave in the "Stages of Change" chapters in Parts I (pages 16–19) and II (pages 80–83).*

1. Contemplation Ladder

Please circle the *one* number on the ladder that most closely describes your thoughts and feelings about quitting smoking today.

10	I have decided to quit smoking.
9	
8	I am close to making a decision to quit smoking.
7	
6	I am thinking about quitting smoking, but I still have not made any definite plans.
5	
4	I am thinking about cutting down on my smoking, but I am not thinking about quitting smoking.
3	
2	I might have a problem with smoking, but I do not intend to cut down or quit now.
1	
0	I do not have a problem with smoking, and I do not intend to cut down or quit now.

2. Preparation Ladder

Please circle the *one* number on the ladder that most closely describes your thoughts and feelings about quitting smoking today.

10	I have decided to cut down on my smoking or to quit, and I have already taken action.
9	
8	I have decided to cut down on my smoking or to quit, and I expect to take action within one week.
7	
6	I have decided to cut down on my smoking or to quit, and I expect to take action within one month.
5	
4	I have decided to cut down on my smoking or to quit, and I expect to take action within one year.
3	
2	I have decided to cut down on my smoking or to quit—someday.
1	
0	I do not intend to cut down on my smoking or to quit.

3. Action Ladder

Please circle the *one* number on the ladder that most closely describes how actively you are working *today* on quitting smoking or preventing a relapse.

10	I do something effective every day to cut down, quit, or prevent a relapse.
9	
8	I have done something effective today to cut down, quit, or prevent a relapse.
7	
6	I have done something effective within the last week to cut down, quit, or prevent a relapse.
5	
4	I have done something effective within the last month to cut down, quit, or prevent a relapse.
3	
2	I once took action to cut down, quit, or prevent a relapse, but I have not done so in more than one month.
1	
0	I have *never* taken any action to cut down, quit, or prevent a relapse.

4. Abstinence Ladder

Please circle the *one* number on the ladder that most accurately describes how much you are smoking right now or how long it has been since your last cigarette.

10	I have not smoked in more than one year.
9	
8	I have not smoked in the last year.
7	
6	I have not smoked in the last thirty days.
5	
4	I have not smoked in the last seven days.
3	
2	I smoked less this week than I used to.
1	
0	I am smoking as much as or more than ever.

5. Maintenance Ladder

Please circle the *one* number on the ladder that most accurately describes the *longest* you have ever gone without smoking a cigarette since you became a regular smoker.

10	More than five years
9	
8	Two years
7	
6	Three months
5	
4	One week
3	
2	One day
1	
0	One hour

6. Relapse Ladder

Mark this ladder *only* if you did not smoke today.

Please circle the *one* number on the ladder that best describes how close you are to smoking again.

10	I no longer consider smoking again.
9	
8	I rarely consider smoking again.
7	
6	I occasionally consider smoking again.
5	
4	I frequently consider smoking again.
3	
2	I intend to smoke again.
1	
0	I have not yet started smoking again, but I have had a cigarette in my hand *within the last week* and almost smoked it.

Summary: Stages of Change Ladders

Record here the number you circled on each ladder. Go back to the charts on pages 19 and 83 and fill in your scores for Part I and Part II. Then fill in your scores for Part III (pages 167–170). The higher the numbers, the more progress you are making.

Date		PART I	PART II	PART III
1.	Contemplation *(Thinking about quitting)*	____	____	____
2.	Preparation *(Making a decision to quit)*	____	____	____
3.	Action *(Taking action to quit)*	____	____	____
4.	Abstinence *(Staying quit now)*	____	____	____
5.	Maintenance *(My experience of staying quit)*	____	____	____
6.	Relapse *(Making sure I stay quit)*	____	____	____

How have you moved up the ladders from one part to the next? Has your Preparation score remained high all the way through? How do your scores now compare with your previous scores? How close are you to relapse?

How long did it take to finish Part II compared with Part I?

You might want to review your scores on these ladders every month. Regular self-evaluation can help you identify your continued progress and your potential for relapse.

– 3 –

History of Addiction Treatment

Treatment of nicotine dependence has evolved over the years from experience gained in treating alcohol and other drug dependencies. Once nicotine was accepted as an addictive substance, addiction specialists began turning their attention to it. Smoking, which had generally been considered a social, medical, or public health problem, began to be considered an addiction problem as well. Therefore, understanding the development of alcohol and drug dependence treatment can help you understand why this program treats nicotine dependence in this way.

For most of human history, dependence on alcohol or other chemicals has been treated as a moral, social, or legal problem. The Bible relates the story of Noah getting drunk; Egyptian papyrus scrolls more than five thousand years old describe the problems of people getting drunk in the beer halls. In each of the last few centuries, authors and playwrights have written about alcoholics and have told their stories. Shakespeare wrote about Falstaff; Charles Dickens depicted several alcoholics, including children. Émile Zola wrote about the social consequences of alcoholism in nineteenth-century France and described delirium tremens (d.t.'s) in his book *L'Assommoir (The Dram Shop)*. William Faulkner, Tennessee Williams, Ernest Hemingway, and Dylan Thomas all recounted tales of alcoholism (including their own).

In 1792, Philippe Pinel, the doctor in charge of the Salpêtrière in Paris, the prison for the insane and demented, released the prisoners and began treating them like medical patients. He believed that they had a sickness of the brain and that they could not control their bizarre behavior. These brain diseases included seizure disorders, hysteria, mental retardation, lunacy, and alcoholism.

In America, the Temperance movement began as soon as Europeans began establishing colonies. Several of the colonies were founded by strict religious orders that did not allow alcohol. The Temperance movement strengthened in the 1840s with the Washington Revival, a movement that saw the alcoholic as a morally ill person in need of care and spiritual treatment. It established a Recovery Home in Boston where alcoholics could live until they were back on their feet.

Around this time the American Association for the Cure of Inebriates was founded. It established homes and asylums, treated alcoholics with kindness, and sought to cure them of their "immoral behavior." There was no government support for this movement, so all the association's work was based on charitable contributions. When the depression of 1873 hit, funds were depleted and it was no longer able to provide these services.

Following World War I, the Temperance movement became the Prohibition movement. Instead of recommending and preaching abstinence as the Temperance supporters did, Prohibition supporters wanted abstinence to be made the law of the land. Starting in the Midwest, more and more people began to see the total prohibition of alcohol manufacture, sale, and consumption as the solution to alcoholism and all of America's social problems. The Volstead Act of 1919 prohibited the sale of intoxicating liquors (defined as any beverage containing more than one-half of 1 percent alcohol). Total prohibition of alcohol use throughout the United States became law in January 1920 as Constitutional Amendment XVIII. During Prohibition (1919–33), per capita consumption of alcohol did decrease (in spite of the contention of some that it increased), but the criminal activity that it engendered was more than society could handle. In December 1933, Amendment XXI repealed Prohibition.

In the 1930s organized treatment for alcoholism as we know it first began. Around 1933 a hospital in Seattle and one in Portland, Oregon, began using aversion therapy, which was first researched in the Soviet Union in the 1920s. Willmar State Hospital in Minnesota established a ward for the treatment of inebriates. Bill Wilson, a stockbroker, and Robert Smith, a physician, founded Alcoholics Anonymous in 1935, and in 1939 completed a book describing their recovery.

Hazelden, a residential treatment center in Center City, Minnesota, was the first freestanding center to incorporate the principles of Alcoholics Anonymous into a professional treatment program. It helped establish the "Minnesota Model" of therapy for alcoholism in the 1940s and launched the era of private hospital treatment for addictions.

Beginning in 1951, Dr. Vincent Dole of the Rockefeller Institute researched the use of methadone as a treatment for heroin addiction; soon, methadone maintenance centers were established around the country. In 1958, Chuck Dederich established Synanon, a recovering community for heroin addicts.

Treatment methods have evolved since that time to include many types of programs. Each program bases its treatment on its assumptions about why people become addicted. Dr. Ken Roy, an addiction specialist in New Orleans, has identified these five "Models of Dependence":

Moral Model
- Cause of the dependence: moral weakness
- Goal of treatment: increased willpower
- Strategy: religious counseling or conversion

Learning Model
- Cause of the dependence: learned habits
- Goal of treatment: self-control through new learning
- Strategy: teach new skills; restructure thinking

Disease Model
- Cause of the dependence: unknown biological factor
- Goal of treatment: complete abstinence
- Strategy: treat the addiction as primary; patient will identify self as "recovering"

Self-Medication Model

- Cause of the dependence: symptom of a primary mental disorder
- Goal of treatment: improved mental functioning
- Strategy: provide psychotherapy and medication treatment for the causative mental disorder; when successful, the compulsive chemical use will cease

Social Model

- Cause of the dependence: environmental influences
- Goal of treatment: improved social functioning
- Strategy: alter environment and coping responses

Most treatment centers today employ an integrative model that combines elements of several of these models. These are also known as "biopsychosocial" or "multivariant" models.

Addiction treatment has moved from the community to the general hospital to the freestanding facility. The standard of treatment in the 1980s became a twenty-eight-day inpatient treatment program that incorporated detoxification, group and individual psychotherapy, education about addictions, family therapy, medical supervision, attendance at Alcoholics Anonymous meetings, and evaluation by a psychiatrist for an underlying psychiatric illness. The standard for treatment today has become a short inpatient stay for detoxification followed by several weeks of residential or outpatient treatment. Much of the current research has focused on determining which treatment approaches are most effective for which patients, with the goal of being more effective with limited resources.

Is outpatient treatment just as effective as inpatient treatment? Experts in the field frequently have strong opinions on this issue. Most doctors and therapists who specialize in addictions believe inpatient treatment is more effective than outpatient treatment. Research comparing inpatient treatment with outpatient is very difficult to do well, and very expensive. The number of valid outcome studies in the literature is limited, and, overall, the results remain inconclusive.

Including nicotine dependence treatment in alcohol and drug addiction treatment programs is a relatively new development. Up to now, smoking has been considered a "right" of psychiatric and chemical dependency treatment patients. Treatment programs have been reluctant to treat (or even address) nicotine dependence for fear that patients would seek treatment elsewhere, that their attention would be distracted from their "main" drug problem, or that the treatment staff would sabotage the treatment because they disagreed with it. In fact, all of these things have happened in various treatment centers that have attempted to go smoke-free without adequate preparation. In the ones that did prepare properly, only minor problems have occurred.

According to the surgeon general, about 11 percent of adult Americans are dependent on alcohol; another 3 percent are dependent on other drugs. About 90 percent of these people are also dependent on nicotine, which means that about 12 percent of adult Americans are dependent on both nicotine and alcohol (or another drug). These percentages have been remarkably constant for many years.

About 24 percent of adult Americans smoke today. (This number has dropped considerably over the past twenty years.) Recall that 12 percent of adult Americans are dependent on tobacco and alcohol or other drugs. Therefore, *half* of all smokers are dependent on alcohol or another drug.

If you believe you have a problem with alcohol or another drug, this would be a good time to get more information. If you are in a group, you can talk about it with your group leader. You could also talk to your doctor, therapist, or spiritual advisor, or you could talk to a friend in Alcoholics Anonymous.

4

Dropping to a Lower Plateau

You should be very proud of yourself for having completed so much work in this program. You have looked at your reasons for wanting to quit smoking, and you have worked to discover which ones are really important. You have identified your triggers for smoking, and you have tried out alternatives to smoking when those triggers occurred. You have faced the fact of your smoking addiction and your dependent behavior. You have confronted the pain that smoking has caused. In other words, you have been learning to take responsibility for your own behavior.

Through all this, you have not been asked to stop smoking, although you have probably been cutting down anyway. By facing the reality of your addiction, you have found it difficult to smoke in your previous pattern. Even if you have not quit yet, smoking is not nearly as enjoyable as it was.

When smokers work the Quit and Stay Quit program, they typically reduce their smoking in the pattern shown on the next page.

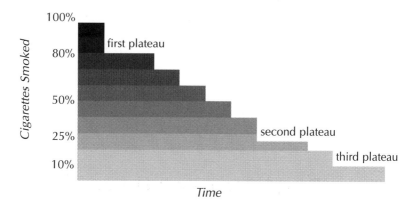

Immediately after starting any cessation program with enthusiasm and high expectations and lots of other people's reasons, most smokers reduce their smoking by about 20 percent—for example, from two and a half packs a day to two packs a day. You were at this point when you made the investment in this book and started the very first chapter.

Smokers who work the Quit and Stay Quit program usually remain at this first plateau for a while. As they continue to work the program aggressively, they stop smoking most of the easily avoidable and unnecessary cigarettes and stabilize at a second plateau, around 25 percent of their previous consumption, or around half a pack a day. They may remain at this plateau for quite a while (sometimes for months) as they integrate what they have achieved and reassess the future. At this level, they can successfully turn down cigarettes they would *like* to smoke but do not *need* to smoke.

With the completion of several of the more difficult chapters in this book, smokers usually drop to the last plateau, where they are smoking only a few cigarettes each day. From here, each reduction in smoking is difficult, but finally, the smoker breaks through and quits altogether.

✎ *Where are you on the graph today? (Mark an "x" and write today's date on the graph on this page.)*

By this time, you are probably on your second plateau or lower, smoking less than 25 percent of what you previously smoked. If you are smoking much more than this, you may have skipped one or more of the chapters in this book or completed them without putting in sufficient effort. If so, this would be a good time to go back over some of the chapters in Parts I and II before proceeding. "Cigarette Smoking Is an Addiction" and "Taking the First Step to Freedom from Smoking" in Part I and "Cigarettes Are Your Best Friend" and "Understanding Your Emotions" in Part II would be good sections to review.

If you are at your second plateau or lower, you are ready to proceed. The time for quitting approaches.

DROPPING TO YOUR LAST PLATEAU

Have you reviewed your journal lately?

If not, go through your reasons to quit smoking in chapter 1 and choose two that stand out as significant today, whether or not they seemed important at the time. Reasons that once seemed compelling may now seem irrelevant, and reasons you previously thought trivial may have become crucial. Rewrite your two reasons in your journal, changing a few words or adding ideas as you feel necessary.

✎ 1. A good reason for me to quit smoking, now and forever, is . . .

✎ 2. Another good reason for me to quit smoking, now and forever, is . . .

Now write down a new reason, one that summarizes these two, plus all the new things you have learned about yourself since you started this program:

✎ The best reason for me to quit smoking, now and forever, is . . .

Now go back to the first two reasons above, and compose a positive statement for each one, starting with "When I am a nonsmoker, . . ."

Then write down a positive restatement of your *best* reason to quit smoking, starting with "When I am a nonsmoker, . . ."

In this chapter, you will review several other completed projects to help you consolidate your gains and get ready to quit altogether.

ADDICTION = TOLERANCE + WITHDRAWAL + BEHAVIORS

In the chapter "Cigarette Smoking Is an Addiction" in Part I (pages 21–46), you looked at your *tolerance* to nicotine. Tolerance means that as time goes by, more and more of the chemical is required to produce the desired effect. Looking back today–now that you are nearly quit— can you identify your tolerance to nicotine?

✎ My tolerance to nicotine is identified by . . .

That chapter also explained that when people become addicted to nicotine, they have symptoms and show signs of *withdrawal* when their intake of nicotine is decreased. Now that you have been experiencing some of this, are you more aware of your withdrawal signs and symptoms?

✎ My withdrawal symptoms (what I feel) from nicotine are . . .

✎ My withdrawal signs (what others observe) from nicotine are . . .

Also in that chapter, you thought about the *behaviors* that go along with your smoking. You examined how you use tobacco ("drug-seeking behaviors") and the things you have done to continue using ("dependent behaviors"). You know a lot more about these behaviors now than you did when you read that chapter originally, so this would be a good time to review what you wrote in your journal about addictions and to make it more complete.

✎ My drug-seeking behaviors have been . . .

✎ My dependent behaviors have been . . .

It would be easy to turn to the next page without actually reviewing the addiction chapter. *Please do not make this error.* Facing your addiction, knowing it, and accepting it form the foundation of this program.

Reviewing and redoing the addiction chapter (pages 21–46) could be crucial to your success.

✎ After your review, please take the time to complete this sentence:

I know I am addicted to cigarettes because . . .

TRIGGERS

"Triggers" are the events and objects in your environment that make you want to smoke. Back when you first worked on this material in Part I, you may have identified such triggers as seeing someone else light up a cigarette, smelling tobacco smoke, feeling hungry, feeling full, or seeing a billboard advertising your brand of cigarettes.

Take this opportunity to reread the chapter "Taking the First Step to Freedom from Smoking," and look over the "Times I Want a Cigarette" section (pages 54–59) and the examples you listed. How many of them are still a problem? Which ones have you discovered since you last worked on that project? Which new ones have appeared as you approach the day when you will smoke your last cigarette?

✎ *In your journal, list five situations when you still feel a strong urge to smoke.*

Now review the things you are doing to avoid smoking in each of these situations. Which ones have been working and which ones haven't? Can you get some new ideas from someone who is going through the program with you? From your sponsors and supporters in Nicotine Anonymous? From the members of a group you are in? From a therapist or counselor? From your doctor? From a nonsmoker who quit recently? From someone close to you?

Go back over some of the previous chapters and see if there is something you missed that might help you now. Review the alternatives to smoking you recorded in the chapter "Understanding Your Emotions" (Part II), pages 115–128. Have you forgotten to use some of them? Do some of them suggest other alternatives?

Have you thought of alternatives that you were unwilling to try? Perhaps you thought they were silly or beneath you or too expensive. Now is the time to use every tool you can find to push cigarettes out of your life. Don't be afraid of any alternative. What you have done in the past did not work well enough; now is the time to try something else. Be willing to do whatever it takes. *You must be willing to go to any lengths to succeed.*

The Big Book of Alcoholics Anonymous reminds alcoholics who are struggling to stay sober that "half measures availed us nothing." So it is with your effort to quit smoking. This is not the time to rely on a weak or convenient alternative instead of a strong but difficult one. You have already quit smoking the cigarettes that were easy to quit (and most of the others as well). All that remains are the last few cigarettes that you have held on to so tightly. Today, you must use your most powerful tools.

✎ *For each of the five trigger situations that you described, list three or four exceptionally good alternatives that can work for you.*

Does this seem to be a lot of work? Have you skipped over some material because it seemed like too much effort? Have you begun wishing for an easier way to quit smoking?

These are normal thoughts. If you could have quit smoking easily or without much effort, you would have done so long ago. If you are still smoking, you owe it to yourself to keep on working.

TAKING ACTION

Starting today, choose two alternatives to smoking that you will emphasize each day. Of course, you can use *all* your alternatives, but *concentrate* on two each day.

At the end of each day, decide which ones were effective and which ones were not. Make notes in your journal, and each day plan to improve. Share your successes and your failures with people who are important to you—friends, family, co-workers, members of your group, supporters in Nicotine Anonymous—and each day get a little closer to quitting.

✎ *In your journal, list names of people with whom you can share your successes.*

Are there still cigarettes that seem impossible to turn down or avoid? Make a list of them, like this:

- the one at lunch with my co-workers on a particularly busy day
- the one after coffee and cake at the bridge club
- the one I light up walking from the parking garage to my office
- the one I really need after my therapy session
- the one I have after sex
- the one I smoke sitting on the toilet in the morning
- the one I have while watching my favorite TV show
- and . . .

Here is a technique you can use to your advantage if you do not *overuse* it. It works like that old football adage: "The best defense is a good offense."

When you enter a situation where you think you might want to smoke or where you can predict that you will smoke, announce that you want to smoke, but that you want to *quit* smoking even more. State that even though you know you are going to want a cigarette, you have decided that you are not going to have one. In this way, you will be creating social pressure on yourself to follow through on your commitment—a powerful addition to your own motivation.

Here is how you can apply this technique to some of the "impossible" situations listed above.

When you sit down at the lunch table and everyone is ready to order, lean forward and announce, "I'm really looking forward to lunch today, but I tell you, I have a heck of a hard time not smoking when lunch is over. I've been doing really well, and I've nearly quit, but I slip up now and again after lunch. Well, I'm not going to have a cigarette after lunch today, even though I know I'm going to want one. Today will be the first day in ages I've had lunch with all of you and didn't smoke." The chances are good that you will not have a cigarette.

During the bridge game, you look forward to the usual cake and coffee, and you also anticipate the accompanying craving for a cigarette. So as the game concludes, tell everyone, "I haven't had a cigarette all day; that may not sound like much to you, but it's been quite a victory for me. Even though I really want one now, I've decided that I'd be better off not smoking, so I'm not going to have one." The likelihood is that you will not smoke this time.

As you leave for work in the morning, knowing that you usually smoke a cigarette between car and office, plan not to smoke by using this technique. Tell your spouse, "You know how I usually smoke a cigarette as I walk from the car to the office? Well, even though I know I'll want one, I'm not going to smoke one today. And I'm going to call you as soon as I get into the office to tell you how well I did." You will probably be successful in not smoking that morning.

As your therapy session concludes, tell your therapist, "I always feel agitated after this session, and I usually smoke a cigarette as soon as I can after I leave. But as you know, I've been trying to quit smoking, and today I'm not going to have a cigarette when I leave here. Instead, I'm going to walk around the building and think out what we've talked about." It will probably work.

Notice that when you use this method you never ask anyone else to keep you away from a cigarette. Don't say, "I know I'll want a cigarette, so nobody give me one and don't let me buy any." *That* approach is destined to fail, because you will not be taking personal responsibility for your own actions. You cannot depend on anyone else, even your most trusted friend, to quit for you.

The "best-defense" technique is easy to use, but you have to plan in advance. To summarize:

1. Use it when you can predict you will want to smoke.
2. It works best in social situations.
3. If you use it too often, it will lose its effectiveness.
4. Long before the time when you know you will want a cigarette, state that you know you will want one but that you are not going to have one.
5. Make a statement of your intentions, not a request for help.
6. Make your statement just once; no one else is all that interested.
7. When you succeed, make a note of it in your journal for future reference.

✎ Some times I could use "best-defense" techniques are when . . .

SO LONG, OLD FRIEND

This chapter may feel tedious or it may feel threatening. You might even feel like giving up right now. There are people who stop working at this point. Facing the ultimate loss of their "friend" is too much for them. If you feel this way, please review the chapter "Cigarettes Are Your Best Friend" in Part II, (pages 91–103).

When you first read that chapter, you might have thought the suggestion that cigarettes were your best friend was pretty farfetched. Please read over that chapter again as well as the corresponding notes you wrote in your journal, and then come back to this section. You might have a different attitude about it today.

As you have worked on understanding your dependence on smoking, you have discovered many new things about your relationship with tobacco. This would be a good time to summarize what you now understand about it.

✎ *In your journal, list ways in which cigarettes have been a **good** friend to you and ways in which cigarettes have become a **false** friend.*

EMOTIONS

At this point in your recovery, you have conquered all of the easily avoided cigarettes. You have broken most of the associations between triggers and smoking. At this stage, most smokers are using their remaining cigarettes to control uncomfortable feelings.

You examined this aspect of your smoking in the chapters "Getting in Touch with the Pain," (pages 105–114) and "Understanding Your Emotions" in Part II, (pages 115–128). Take some time today to review these two chapters to help you understand which feelings you have altered, controlled, exaggerated, minimized, avoided, stuffed, or released with nicotine.

Since you have much less nicotine in your system today than you had when you first worked on that chapter, you will be better able to recognize your feelings today. This may not be comfortable at first, but emotional growth rarely is.

I am now aware that I used cigarettes
to deal with feelings like the following:

FEELING	EFFECTS OF SMOKING ON THAT FEELING
Anger	*It keeps the anger stuffed inside me.*
Resentment	*It lets me avoid having to face the person I resent.*
Depression	*It helps me forget about how hopeless I feel.*
Rejection	*It lets me be part of the gang.*
Humiliation	*It makes me look cool and I don't have to deal with the truth.*

THE LAST PLATEAU

You have successfully reviewed the work you have done in this program and have contributed important new insights. In the next chapter, you will set a Quit Date (if you have not already done so) and say good-bye to tobacco.

✎ I know I am ready to leave my old friend tobacco because . . .

5

Finishing Your Last Pack

You are approaching the point on your journey of recovery when you will crush out your last cigarette. That event may have already occurred, or it may occur tomorrow, next week, next month, or next year. In this program, we recognize that the exact moment when you smoke that last cigarette is not especially important. It is far more important that when you quit, you *stay* quit. The real work of recovery begins *after* you smoke your last cigarette.

Some people get ready to quit gradually, over many weeks; others decide to quit on the spur of the moment. Some cut down a little at a time; others quit all at once. For some people, quitting is a calm, rational decision; for others it is an emotional crisis. Some people need lots of freedom to do things their own way; others prefer to have some structure.

You can quit smoking, whatever type of person you are. If you are like most people, you will do better with a little structure, and this chapter may help. If you do not respond well to structure, this chapter may be no more than interesting reading for you, and you will want to finish your last pack on your own.

Think twice, though, before rejecting the help this book offers. If you could have quit smoking without help, you would have done it long ago.

If you think you will do better with some structure, consider following the plan described in this chapter.

MAKING A ONE-WEEK PLAN

Choose one pack of cigarettes to be your last.

This plan will help you progress from smoking just a few cigarettes each day to quitting for good. It will include all your regular activities, any unusual events you can foresee, and all the stressful periods you can predict.

During this week, your goal will be to smoke no more than three cigarettes each day and to plan when to smoke them.

Start the week by taking your current pack of cigarettes and dumping them all out. Save the empty package. This will be your last pack.

Each morning, take the exact number of cigarettes you plan to smoke that day and put them into the empty package. Carry it around until the time you planned to smoke occurs; then you can smoke. Save the empty package for the next day.

No fair bumming a smoke from someone else. We are getting down to brass tacks now.

Each evening during the week, review some of the material in this book. If more points come to mind, add them in your journal. Discuss your work with someone else you care about, someone who understands what you are going through. You will benefit from all the help you can get.

Each evening, make a note of several alternatives to smoking that you can emphasize during the next day. Write them on an index card and carry the card with you. Refer to it frequently. You could also write some alternatives to smoking, some affirmative thoughts, or some inspirational quotations on the back of a business card or half an index card. Slip the card behind the cellophane of your cigarette pack. Whenever you take out your cigarette pack, look over the comments on the card before you smoke a cigarette.

Review the chapter "Relaxation Techniques" in Part II (pages 129–135). It describes several methods you can use to reduce anxiety. Ask someone who understands these relaxation techniques to help you. You will want to use all your available support systems now. This is your last week of smoking.

Put your plans for this week on the chart on page 193. Refer to the example that shows how to fill in the chart. It contains space to write in when you will work, what you will do for fun and relaxation, time you will spend with your family, other events you know about, problems you anticipate, and when you will allow yourself to smoke a cigarette.

Now choose the exact day on which you plan to quit smoking. Write "Quit Day" on this day on your weekly plan. *Your goal will be not to smoke again, starting on this day.*

Plan to spend some time on this day and on each of the next few days sharing your feelings with people you care about. Discuss with them the journey of recovery you have been on, and how important it has been to you. This will be an important day in your life, so plan for it well.

Now make a second one-week plan for the week after your last cigarette (page 194). This week may be a stressful one, so include activities that help you reduce stress and postpone events that you know might be affected by your increased anxiety. (You might be able to move some of these to the week before, since you are planning ahead.)

Include, as before, when you will work, what you will do for enjoyment and relaxation, time you will spend with your family, other items of importance, and any problems you can anticipate. Also write down which cigarettes you *might have* smoked, but will not. This will help you predict when you will be the most anxious.

Later in this chapter, you will learn about writing a "good-bye" letter to "Tobacco," an important ritual in your recovery. Include time for this ritual on your second one-week plan.

Keep several index cards in your pocket or purse on which you have written tried-and-true alternatives and positive affirmations. You might want to buy a pocket-sized book filled with positive affirmations; you can carry it around and refer to it when your motivation begins to wane or when you feel the urge to smoke.

Don't stop now; your goal is in sight.

✎ *In your journal, make some notes on your quitting strategies.*

Sample Weekly Plan (date) to (date)

	Work	Fun	Family	Other	Problems	Cigarette
Monday	8:30–5:00	watch TV with family	play in backyard with kids	call Grandma and Grandpa	tired from work	one right after supper
Tuesday	8:30–5:00	swim with kids	family swim at YMCA	do IRS return	IRS	one while doing IRS tax return
Wednesday	8:30–5:00	bowling 8:00 P.M.	supper at Aunt Stella's 6:00 P.M.	finish IRS return	will be up late	one during and one after bowling
Thursday	8:30–5:00	TV	go for a walk and fly kites	register kids for summer camp	pay bills	morning and afternoon coffee break
Friday	8:30–5:00	go to movies	take family to movies	balance checkbook relaxation exercises	rent due	just one during afternoon coffee break
Saturday	work in garden; water house-plants	read a novel or watch TV	both kids have Little League practice	practice relaxation exercises dinner out	finding a babysitter	one after dinner at the restaurant
Sunday	clean up house	read Sunday paper	church read funnies together	practice relaxation exercises; church committee	work tomorrow	↓ ↓ → none ← →tonight← ↑ ↑
Monday	8:30–5:00	watch TV with family	talk with family about not smoking	relaxation exercises morning, noon, night	ANXIETY!	. . . . QUIT DAY . . . .

First-Week Plan _____ **to** _____

	Work	Fun	Family	Other	Problems	Cigarette

Second-Week Plan _____ to _____

	Work	Fun	Family	Other	Problems	Cigarette

You learned early on in this program not to try to quit until you were ready to quit. If you have worked all these projects and you have made your weekly plans, then you are ready to quit. Follow your plan, rely on the people who support you, accept help from family and friends, and put your plan into action.

If you are a member of a group, keep going to group sessions after you have smoked your last cigarette. Some of the most difficult days lie ahead and your group and group leader can be your strongest sources of support.

If your plan does not succeed, *make a new plan.* Perhaps it was overly enthusiastic or did not take all your stress into account.

This may be a time when you would benefit from some individual counseling. If so, seek out a counselor or therapist with a background in addiction counseling or chemical dependency treatment. He or she will have the best understanding of what you are going through.

Extend your one-week plan if necessary. Now is the time to do whatever is necessary to succeed.

GOOD-BYE TOBACCO—HELLO ME

Now you are ready to finally leave your cigarettes behind and move on to a new way of life. When you are certain that you are ready, read through the rest of this chapter and then return to this spot.

Take some paper and write a letter to Tobacco, telling it good-bye forever. Be as detailed and specific as you can. Make your letter very personal. Rewrite it as many times as necessary until you are satisfied that it expresses your true feelings. Then copy it into your journal so that you have a permanent copy.

It may be hard to write this letter. Cigarettes have been a big part of your life for a long time. You have relied on them to help you in many situations. But now it's time to say good-bye.

On the following pages are some examples of "Good-bye Tobacco" letters that others have written.

Good-bye Cigarettes and Tobacco,

Now that I have been completely free of you for the last few days, I can wholeheartedly write this good-bye letter. I had to taste that freedom from you first before I was convinced that I could and should live without you. As I look back on our relationship, I think of you as an anchor who kept me company and steadied me when I was scared, hurt, lonely, impatient, and frustrated. But like an anchor, you kept me in the same place.

In the beginning, I probably struggled a little more against you or at least thought I was in control. Instead, you showed me I wasn't going anywhere without you—which meant I wasn't going anywhere at all. Your victory was almost complete, for I did give up trusting in my future, in fact. My thoughts and dreams of the future turned into nightmares. Those nightmares are what brought me here.

With all the help and support of this group, and my family, I set myself free of you on Sunday, June 22, and I intend to remain free for always.

Sincerely,

Alice

Good-bye Tobacco,

It's been about thirty-five years since I first tried you—when my girlfriend and I would steal cigarettes and matches from her mother and go down to the riverbank to smoke. You tasted terrible, but we felt very grown-up and slightly wicked. Then there was an occasional smoke with older friends in high school.

College was when I really got hooked on you. I used to bum cigarettes from sorority sisters when I didn't have money to buy them. This was in the fifties, when it was cool to smoke—everyone did it.

My dad smoked from the time he was fourteen or so; eventually you killed him with a stroke at sixty-nine. There are so many aunts and uncles on both sides of my family who used you and later paid the price with cancer or strokes. My mother smoked during my teens and twenties and later quit. I felt justified smoking at home. After all, if she did it, why shouldn't I?

Then I married, and Jack smoked too, so we were very compatible. Later, when the children came along (three in four years), it was so nice to relax with a cigarette whenever I had free time. We moved around a lot in the first thirteen years of marriage—ten houses in five states, plus Jack was a traveling salesman—so you really *were* my friend and comforter with all those stresses and strains.

I've tried to leave you before. The first time was the summer of 1968, when I quit for a year—until the summer of '69, when we heard we were being transferred from Texas back to New Jersey and we didn't want to go. The last time I quit was ten years ago. That lasted almost two years. Jack started again when a cousin came here to work for him. This guy was a heavy smoker, and Jack and I both succumbed.

Now here I am, forty-nine years old, and I'm tired of being addicted to you, Tobacco, and having you dictate the shape my life will take. I don't want to choose my friends on the basis of whether they smoke.

I don't want to have to avoid going places because I can't smoke there.

I don't want to have to rush to the store at 10 P.M. to get my fix.

I don't want my children to see me smoke.

I'm tired of putting up with all the aches and pains associated with smoking.

I can't believe how much I've been fooling myself all these years with you, Tobacco, clinging to you like a life raft, when in actuality you are the very opposite of life. You are *death* just as surely as night follows day. They should require a skull and crossbones on cigarette packs.

So after wasting all those years and all that money, I'm giving you up for good, Tobacco. It isn't going to be easy to break this hold you have on me, but I'll just take one day at a time, or better still, one urge to smoke at a time, and I *will* make it, because my life depends on it.

Sincerely,

Trish

Good-bye Tobacco,

Good-bye Marlboros, Marlboro Lights, Kools, and Carltons. Good-bye cigars at Uncle Bob's. Good-bye soft-packs and crush-proof boxes, Zippos and Bics, menthols and filters. I never want to know you again.

You were a good friend to me at times. I enjoyed you, and you made me feel good, but in the end, you robbed me of my endurance and whittled away at my self-respect. I lived with you for much too long, but I'm waking up today, and today our affair is over.

I first got to know you when I was about nine years old. I stole a cigarette from my parents' coffee table and lit up behind the holly tree. Only you and I know how sick I got! I was far too embarrassed to tell anyone about it. I coughed and sputtered and felt queasy; you made my head swim, and I felt giddy. I sort of liked that feeling, even though it was a little scary. But I also felt very grown-up. I remember tossing my head back, like the movie stars did, and blowing out the smoke. You were starting to hook me even then, weren't you?

After finishing that cigarette, I remember being so frightened I would be discovered that I buried the cigarette butt and the matches and scattered all the ashes.

And today I am going to bury you forever. I will scatter your ashes so that you will never dirty up my life again.

I remember that after I smoked you that first time, I ran back into the house and brushed my teeth a dozen times so no one would notice the foul smell you left on my breath. I even changed my clothes so that no one would smell the smoke on them. I scrubbed my face in case you had left a tell-tale smudge.

And today I am cleaning myself up for the rest of my life. I do not need you anymore, Tobacco, so good-bye.

There have been lots of times when I relied on you. When I would get nervous—especially when I'd have to give a talk or present something to a supervisor—you would help me to calm down. I have learned, though, that I can conquer that sort of anxiety without using chemicals, including you. And by doing that, I have gained self-respect and the respect of my friends. I will not need your help ever again to calm down.

When I felt bored or had to wait in line or in stalled traffic, you kept my hands occupied. I always felt that someone just waiting looked vulnerable and dependent. Smoking a cigarette made me look calm and in control (I thought). Now I realize that I was the one who was dependent, dependent on you. I am learning to handle boredom and frustration—they are part of life. And I intend to live.

Lately I have needed two or three cigarettes to get that giddy feeling I experienced so long ago after one or two puffs, but I can still get it. Now I know that this is called "tolerance," and it means that I am addicted to you. Well, you won the addiction fight—I am addicted. But I am going to win the smoking fight. Even though I *am* addicted to you, and always will be, I do not ever have to smoke again.

You provided me with convenient excuses for many years. When I got tired of studying in college, I could take a break to smoke. When my "In" box at work got overwhelming, I could stop to have a cigarette. If an argument with my wife started to develop, I could delay it (and sometimes avoid it) by searching for you, taking out a cigarette, and lighting it up. I realize now that for years, one reason I could not quit smoking was my fear of such situations.

I now know that I can deal with these situations without you. You never helped me as much as I thought. If I chose you over studying, no one else did my studying for me—I *still* had to go back to the books eventually. If I chose you over working, no one else did my work for me—I *still* had to get it done. (And many times I had to stay late to complete it.) Sure, I avoided some spats with my wife by smoking—but look where it got me!

You have manipulated my life, and I am sick and tired of it. No more will I let you tell me where to sit in a restaurant; no more will you force me to get up in the middle of a movie to go to the lobby for a smoke. No more will I let you tell me who to spend my time with or for how long.

I've wasted so much money on you! And for what? It's all burned up! That's crazy. I have been smoking nearly three packs a day lately—two entire cartons a week. Even buying you mostly at a discount place (and occasionally from a vending machine when I get really desperate), I'm spending $500 a year on you. And to think of all the trousers I've burned holes in, sofas and chairs I've singed, shirts and jackets I've dropped ashes on! My unnecessary dry-cleaning bills could pay a month's rent.

The worst thing about that is, I've burned holes in *other people's* things. Even though I've paid to patch up your damage, things are never the same again. It's easier to patch up a hole in a sofa than to patch up a friendship.

I decided to see how many times I have experienced your effect. I have smoked you for twenty-five years, averaging about two packs a day:

- 2 packs x 365 days = 730 packs a year
- 730 packs a year x 25 years = 18,250 packs
- 18,250 packs x 20 cigarettes in a pack = 365,000 cigarettes
- 365,000 cigarettes x 10 puffs each = 3,650,000 puffs

I have experienced your effect at least three and a half million times! You have really controlled me—but not anymore. As of this day, I declare myself free of you.

You have robbed me of my health. You make me cough in the morning, wheeze half the day, lose time from work with allergies, colds, and flu, and limit my endurance. I can barely get up two flights of stairs these days, huffing and puffing all the way. When I have sex, I get short of breath—but you have got me so addicted, the first thing I want after sex is a cigarette!

You took my Aunt Lou from me prematurely; she died of lung cancer last year. Years ago, lung cancer was rare in women; two years ago, it was the second-leading type of cancer in women. Now, they tell me, it is the most common kind. I hope you are happy with the misery and pain you have caused.

You addicted my father and added to his heart disease. He is still alive, but no thanks to you. He had a heart attack, and if he had never smoked, it might not have happened. In spite of his heart attack, he went back to smoking. How powerful you are! I am totally unable to help him quit smoking, and it makes me feel weak and ashamed. All I can do is change myself; perhaps my father will choose to follow my example. I will give you up, and I will show him that he can give you up too.

You play on our human weaknesses—how did you get to be so clever? Businesses sell you and make a profit. Lawmakers protect you to maintain power. Kids smoke you to look older. Older folks smoke you to look younger. Everyone uses you to feel the rush of your nicotine and to push reality a little bit further into the background. Where did you learn how to do all that?

Well, Tobacco, I have experienced you for the last time. I choose never to smoke again. I will not use snuff, chewing tobacco, a pipe, cigar, or cigarette ever again. I don't need you, and I don't need your chemical rush. I will rely on my own strength, creativity, and resourcefulness from now on.

I am only now realizing how I pursued you, never getting enough, always willing to do any number of insane things to keep you close. Do you remember the time I decided to quit using you and went deer hunting with just one pack of cigarettes? I said, "When I've finished smoking these, I'm finished." Boy, *I* was nearly finished! After spending a day and a half without cigarettes, I drove forty miles out of the woods to the first gas station and bought a carton of cigarettes. I smoked just about an entire pack on the way back—so much that I got light-headed and had to pull off to the side of the road for a while. You had me fooled, Tobacco, into thinking I was in control. What I have learned is that to regain control over my life, I need to give up control of my smoking addiction. By accepting that I can't control you, I will be able to control me.

I know that the days and weeks and years ahead will be full of your attempts to get me back. I will make plans now on how to resist your temptations. I will continue to study myself and learn more about why I wanted you so much for so long. My work isn't over—it is just beginning, really—but I feel good about what I have done, and I am not afraid of the future.

I know that other people still remain caught in your clutches. I am sorry for them because now I see that I could have escaped from you long ago if I hadn't been so afraid of knowing myself. You kept me locked in a prison, but I always had the key to the door—I just didn't know it! I hope I can be of help to someone else trapped in the same dungeon; I will show them that they, too, possess the key to their freedom. It will make me very happy to help someone else escape from you.

So good-bye, Tobacco. I relied on you for years, and you ended up hurting me. Now I am going to leave you behind.

Sincerely,

Bob

When you are all done with your letter saying "Good-bye Tobacco," write another letter saying "Hello Me." Here are some examples:

Hello Linda,

I didn't really get around to writing this letter until just a few minutes ago. I spent all my time saying good-bye to Tobacco, and I didn't have any time left to say hello to myself. I guess in the past I've done that—not take care of me. Well, that's going to stop now, and I'm going to take care of me.

I just want to thank all of you in the group for being there when I needed you. I can't believe I've told you all those things about myself; even more, I can't believe you didn't all just throw me out of here—but I'm glad you didn't, because I've never felt better in my whole life than I do now, and I couldn't have done it without this group.

I now know that I was dying, and that I was killing myself, only slowly—but not anymore, thanks to all of you and this program.

So I guess all I can say is thank you, Linda, and I love you now.

Sincerely,

Linda

Hello Katy,

It's been almost three whole days since you smoked a cigarette. You're doing great and I'm proud of you. Already you have more pep and energy and more incentive to get off your rear and *do* things.

These past eight years since you resumed smoking have been like a long downhill slide into a stronger and stronger addiction, with all the accompanying physical and emotional pain—that's why stopping that slide and turning your life around is such a positive step.

You are worth saving, and you have a lot of people who love and support you and will give you all the emotional help you need if you feel yourself slipping.

So just hang in there and look forward to the time when you have clean lungs and a body that's no worse than any other *nonsmoker's* your age.

It's going to be so nice to face the future without that smoking albatross around your neck dictating to you.

You are free now, and you want to stay that way, so keep up the good work.

Sincerely,

Katy

Hello Mike,

It's good to see you with a clear head and clear eyes. No more red, watery, bleary eyes for you. It's good to see you looking positive and enthusiastic about life. It's nice to have you and your clothes smell so clean and fresh. Hey, what's different about you? Oh, you quit smoking! Good for you!

I guess you didn't realize how much your smoking was affecting you and the people around you. I guess you know now. It's probably kind of tough to face that sort of stuff, but you've done it, and you are continuing to do it. Whoever would have thought that you had that kind of gumption? Not you, that's for sure.

What will you be like as a nonsmoker? Pretty much the same, I guess. But there will always be a little part of you that says, "Wow, I really did something back then." And maybe that knowledge will give you strength for accomplishing other challenges in the future.

People have been telling you for so long that you ought to quit, but this time, you decided for yourself. This time, you're quitting for *your* reasons, not for anyone else's. So this time, the chances are good that you will *stay* quit.

I sure hope so. Each time you've quit for a while and then started up again, you've felt like you couldn't do anything right.

It's a lousy feeling to try and fail, try and fail. But this time, it looks like you are doing this right. You've got all your ducks in a row, and it looks like you mean business. This time, I think you will make it.

You get all the credit. No one did it for you. You can really be proud of yourself.

I think it will be easier now for people to get to know you. Some of them might actually like you. I know that I do now.

Just keep taking it one day at a time.

Sincerely,

Mike

After participating in a Quit and Stay Quit group for weeks, one man came to see how his smoking had become his primary relationship. He had begun to understand how he had replaced his human relationships with smoking; how he had become more intimate with his cigarettes than he had ever been with a woman; how, in fact, cigarettes had become his lover. He could not adequately describe his feelings in a Good-bye Tobacco letter, so he wrote this poem.

There she was
All wrapped in a gown of
Silver accentuated by strips of blue,
Adorned with an emerald . . .
I smiled with wild anticipation.
Not a word was spoken as I removed her silver top.
Panting rapidly
I gently stroked every inch of her lovely white body
While inhaling her aromatic fragrance
Lighting her fire with mad passion

Sucking on her orifice
Tasting her sweet addictive juices.
I felt my hormones and adrenaline
Coursing through my body.
I had to have her again and again.
After a while my craving was satisfied.
And she lay exhausted,
Broken in the ashtray.

—"LOVE AFFAIR" BY L. B.

Your letters can take any form you wish—prose, poetry, story, play, song, speech, prayer, myth, conversation—it's up to you. The point is to use pen and paper to organize your thinking, summarize your feelings, and demonstrate your commitment to a smoke-free life.

You may need to live with yourself tobacco-free for a while before you are ready to write your own letters. Even if you're not completely ready, begin writing down some ideas. Many people find that once they start, their thoughts come flowing out.

You will want to work on your letters for some time. After you think they are all done, put them away for a while and come back to them. New ideas will come to you and you will find things to add or revise.

After you have worked out the drafts of your letters, rewrite them on the pages of your journal or notebook. These letters will be a big step toward freedom for you.

When you are satisfied with your letters and when you have not smoked in more than a week, set aside some time to read your letters and discuss them with someone you trust who has supported you in your efforts to quit smoking. If you are part of a group, you can do this in one of your group meetings.

Choose a day and time when you and your supporter can be together for a while without being disturbed. Tell this person what it has meant for you to experience addiction to cigarettes and what it is like to be entering recovery.

Ask for patience and understanding. Describe how this has been a difficult journey for you. Share your thoughts and feelings. Ask your supporter to really listen to what you have to say. Explain what an important moment this is and request that it be treated with respect.

Then read your letters out loud.

You will experience tremendous relief. You will truly feel that you will never smoke again.

But remember how cunning, baffling, and powerful addictive chemicals are. This moment is your Commencement, which means that you have *commenced,* or begun, the next phase of your life, your life as a recovering person. Your work is not completed; rather, your new life is just beginning.

The rest of this book deals with this new life that lies ahead.

✎ *On a separate sheet of paper, write down some notes to help you prepare to write your letters.*

– 6 –

Making a Relapse Prevention Plan

Relapsing means that the underlying disease takes hold again. In diabetes, relapsing means that the blood sugar goes out of control again. In rheumatoid arthritis, relapsing means that the pain and stiffness in the joints are no longer adequately relieved by medications. In leukemia, relapsing means that the tumor cells can no longer be controlled by the treatment.

In your cigarette addiction, as with all chemical addictions, relapsing means that the compulsion to use chemicals overwhelms your efforts to continue recovering. The relapse starts when it becomes *possible* to use chemicals again; this may occur long before the person actually uses the chemical. The relapse process can be halted if the person understands it and is willing to take action.

An alcoholism relapse might start when the recovering alcoholic goes into a bar to use the telephone—it then becomes *possible* to drink. A cocaine relapse might start when the recovering cocaine addict drives into the old neighborhood with $200 in the glove compartment—it then becomes *possible* to use cocaine. A smoking relapse might start when the recovering smoker wanders into a smoke shop looking for a gift, or picks up someone else's cigarettes that were sitting on the table "to return them," or buys a carton of cigarettes for someone else while shopping—it then becomes *possible* to smoke again.

Some people like to use the term "slip" to mean that they started to smoke again, as in "I was doing real well; I hadn't had a cigarette in three months until I slipped." *There are no "slips" in addictive diseases—only "relapses."* If you relapse to smoking, you have not been paying enough attention to your recovery. "Slipping" implies that it was no fault of your own, that it could have happened to anybody. This is rarely the case. Relapsing smokers are not forced to smoke against their will or fooled into smoking. Relapsing means that the addiction is in charge again.

"Slip" stands for "Something Lousy I Planned." Relapses are generally premeditated; when relapsing smokers look closely, they can usually see where they set themselves up to relapse. In Alcoholics Anonymous, "slip" stands for "Sobriety Loses Its Priority." In your case, "slip" stands for "Smoking Levies Its Price."

In this chapter, you will have an opportunity to look at times in the past when you relapsed and discover how you may have set yourself up to relapse. You will also develop a relapse prevention plan for yourself to make relapse less likely.

It is normal to want to skip this section. "I no longer have any desire to smoke," you may say, "so this relapse business is a waste of time." Certainly, you do not intend to relapse. However, the research data show that most people who quit start smoking again within a year. Do not abandon your firm intention to stay quit and your determination not to relapse, but recognize reality: addictions are chronic diseases that are never "cured" and that can never be said to be completely gone. Even people with years of abstinence sometimes relapse.

What will help you avoid a relapse? Honest self-examination, an open mind, willingness, strong motivation, and a solid recovery plan—these will all make relapse less likely, but they will not guarantee that you will not relapse.

No matter how long an alcoholic stays sober or a heroin addict stays clean or a cigarette addict stays off cigarettes, the seeds of tolerance and withdrawal remain within. They are dormant now, but they can germinate if the climate is right. In spite of a strong recovery plan and years of a chemical-free life, there will be times when the craving to smoke will sneak up on you. It is for these times you need to have a relapse prevention plan.

Developing a relapse prevention plan does not mean you are anticipating a relapse. It means that you are aware that relapses do occur, and that to be one of the successes, you must accept that some people don't succeed. *Failing to plan is planning to fail.*

The tightrope walker doesn't *plan* to fall off the rope, but has a net below just in case. The tightrope walker doesn't plan to fall, but has a plan in case of a fall.

The anesthesiologist preparing for surgery doesn't *plan* to have the patient's heart stop during surgery, but checks the cardiac defibrillator before surgery just in case. The anesthesiologist doesn't plan to have the patient's heart stop, but has a plan in case it does stop.

You are not *planning* to start smoking again. You have put a great deal of effort into this program already. You need a plan to deal with those times when you will be tempted to smoke again and just in case you do start smoking again.

You should have two parts to your relapse prevention plan:

- *Part 1:* What to do if you have not yet started smoking but feel that you could start anytime soon.
- *Part 2:* What to do if you do start smoking again.

STOPPING THE BUS *(BUILDING UP TO SMOKE)*

Have you ever wondered why cigarette companies spend so much money on advertising? Did you think it was to support the hungry children of advertising executives? Probably not. More likely, it's to sell cigarettes. The *New England Journal of Medicine* reported that in 1983, the tobacco companies spent $1.5 billion on cigarette promotion in the United States and that the twelve pages of cigarette advertising in a typical issue of *Newsweek* magazine cost $1 million. In 1987, the tobacco companies spent $2.4 billion on tobacco promotion. In 1994, they spent more than $3.5 billion. It looks as though somebody wants to convince you to smoke and is willing to pay a lot of money to do it.

These promotions (advertising, sponsoring music and sports events, cigarette and smokeless tobacco giveaways, franchising the name and image of the cigarette product, and so on) are obviously targeted at people who will purchase and smoke cigarettes. There are only three types of people who will ever smoke cigarettes:

1. presmokers (someone who has never smoked, or has only experimented with cigarettes, but who will become a regular smoker)
2. smokers
3. former smokers

Most *presmokers* are teenagers. The ads carry the message that smoking makes them part of the crowd, grown-up, and independent. One ad is not likely to convince a kid to start smoking, but hundreds and hundreds of ads, over several years, become very convincing.

The *smokers* tend to buy the same type of cigarette consistently. Smokers tend to be loyal to their brand, rarely switching. However, the cigarette companies figure that it's worth their effort to try. After all, these people are already smoking (and buying) cigarettes, and if they *can* be pried loose from their current brand and get attached to a new one, they will probably be loyal to it for some time.

You are in the third category. You used to smoke, but you don't smoke today. The cigarette companies are not as interested in your health as they are in your money. So they are going to try to get you back. You are now fair game, and every company is interested in you.

What will they say to you to try to get you back? You now know that if you smoke *one* cigarette, you are likely to continue smoking. They must know it too. So what are they likely to do to get you to try that first one?

They will appeal to your imagination, play on your fantasies, and exploit your romance with cigarettes. They will picture cigarettes as healthy (using a ruggedly handsome cowboy in the fresh air of Montana or a svelte athletic woman reclining after a workout). You know cigarettes are unhealthy, but you would like to fantasize that they are okay, so you might be attracted to these images.

They will portray smokers as sophisticated (using a picture of a tuxedoed young man and a designer-gowned young woman sampling caviar at a nightclub, or packaging the cigarettes in an elegant box). You know that sophistication is in the person, not the cigarette, but you might be tempted to believe that a cigarette helps, and you might be tantalized by these illusions.

They will picture cigarettes as sensible (offering cents-off coupons, putting twenty-five in a pack instead of twenty, promoting lower-tar and lower-nicotine cigarettes). You know that smoking cigarettes is foolish, but everyone wants to save money and stay healthy, so you might be enticed by these bargains.

As part of your relapse prevention plan, gather twenty or so cigarette ads from magazines, newspapers, and circulars. Include those you spot on billboards and any promotions you see (like Virginia Slims tennis, Winston rodeo circuit, or free boxes of cigarettes given out on street corners).

Evaluate the ads: What are they trying to do? What impulse of mine are they trying to exploit? What fantasy of mine are they stimulating? How are they trying to hook me again?

If you can see through the ads and begin to understand your own fantasies about smoking, you will be better protected from relapse.

Concentrate first on the brand you used to smoke. Collect six or eight ads for it and determine what image the advertising company is trying to project for that particular brand. You felt some attraction to it once—why? Identify at least half a dozen characteristics and write them in your journal.

Here are some suggestions:

very masculine	very feminine
stable and mature	young and spirited
sensible	daring
down-to-earth blue-collar	cosmopolitan white-collar
highly independent	part of the crowd
works every day	so rich he doesn't need to work
outdoor type	urban sophisticate
gets attention by smoking	prefers to be a solitary smoker

✎ The image projected by the brand I used to smoke is . . .

✎ What is there about this image that I was so attracted to?

✎ Why do I want to be like that image?

✎ If I'm really like that, I don't need the cigarette to help me—and if I'm really *not* like that, why am I aspiring to be someone I'm not?

Now look at some of the ads for other brands. Which ones seem to stick in your mind? Which billboard do you seem to recall? If you had switched from your regular brand, what would have been your second choice? What fantasies are the other brands trying to tempt you with? By knowing where they have set traps, you will be better prepared to avoid them.

✎ What impulse of mine are they trying to exploit?

✎ What fantasy of mine are they trying to appeal to?

✎ How are they going to try to hook me again?

Show these ads to a friend who is also working on recovery from smoking and discuss what you have learned from them. If you are working with a group, devote a group session to this part of relapse prevention planning. Be sure to bring part of your advertisement collection with you to that group.

Keep an eye open for the work of Bonnie Vierthaler, an artist who has created satirical collages out of cigarette ads. For example, one of Vierthaler's collages shows an old man with emphysema hacking painfully, underneath the slogan "Kent III taste. Experience it!" Another one shows four monkeys, three of whom are smoking cigarettes, with the headline "3 of 4 Smokers Choose Merit." Another of her Merit collages advertises Merit's crush-proof box—the picture shows a coffin holding a few cigarettes.

You can make some of your own collages—what Vierthaler calls "badvertising." Cut out pictures from magazines or draw your own. Cut and paste them onto cigarette ads so that the ads show the truth, not the fantasy.

If you would like to see some of Vierthaler's work, she will send you a free brochure.

Ms. Bonnie Vierthaler
The Badvertising Institute
195 Congress St.
Portland, ME 04101
(207) 761-4414
(207) 773-3275

DAILY MINI-PROJECTS

Your recovery from smoking addiction is an all-day, every-day affair. Your goal is a lifetime of recovery, achieved one day at a time. At first, you may need to stay clean one hour at a time, or even five minutes at a time. Eventually, it does get *easier,* but it probably will never get *easy.*

Every day for one month after your Quit Day, do a "daily mini-project." In your journal or notebook, write the date and devote a paragraph to one of these mini-projects:

1. How did I fantasize about smoking today?
2. Today, what made me grateful that I am a nonsmoker?
3. How did I strengthen my sobriety from cigarettes today?
4. How close did I come to smoking today?
5. If I had smoked today, what would be happening to me now?
6. What successes did I have today that would not have come to me if I were still smoking?
7. When do I still have a craving for a cigarette?
8. What did I do today to help someone else stay off cigarettes?
9. What did I do to not smoke today?
10. What happened today that made me think about smoking again?
11. What did I learn about myself today?
12. What are my goals for tomorrow?

As you go through your day, make an effort to recognize the times when you used to smoke. For those times when you no longer have a desire to smoke, make a point of pausing and telling yourself, *There were days I would've died for a cigarette right about now; I can hardly believe I'm sitting here with no desire to smoke. Good for me!* For those times when you still want a cigarette, pause and praise yourself for not smoking: *I really want to smoke right now, but I know if I smoke just one,*

I'll be back smoking as much as ever in no time. So I'm not going to smoke. Good for me!

Identify the times when you still want a cigarette and write them down. Be as specific as possible; for example, "when I have something to eat" is not specific enough. Score each time on a scale of 0 to 10, with 0 meaning "no desire to smoke" and 10 meaning "I can't think of anything except smoking." By recognizing when you most want a cigarette, you will be better equipped to deal with the craving.

Here is an example of getting more specific than "when I have something to eat."

I still want a cigarette when I have something to eat . . .

❑ after a big meal in a fancy restaurant
❑ during a hectic business lunch at work
❑ after supper with the family
❑ with coffee and sweet rolls in the morning
❑ when I'm eating in an airport
❑ when I'm taking my mother-in-law to lunch
❑ with pizza at the baseball game
❑ when I have to wait for a table in a restaurant
❑ when I don't like what I'm served

❑ and _____

✎ *You can get even more specific.*

I still want a cigarette when I have something to eat . . .

❑ with Italian/Chinese/German/Mexican/French food
❑ with sweet/salty/spicy/crunchy/bland/greasy foods
❑ with the appetizers/salad/entree/dessert
❑ when the dining room is noisy/quiet/deserted/bright/dark
❑ when I'm especially hungry/especially full
❑ when I have a mixed drink/a beer/a glass of wine/a soft drink/coffee
❑ with a large/small/medium meal
❑ with a hamburger/cheeseburger/hot dog/sandwich/taco/egg roll

❑ and _____

Now make a similar list dealing with working, having fun, staying at home, going out on social occasions, driving in the car, and every other occasion when you used to smoke. Write your lists in your journal, and review them frequently.

After you write your lists, score each item from 0 to 10 based on how much you still want to smoke in that situation. When you find some eights, nines, and tens, pay special attention—these are the situations in which you are most likely to relapse. You must either avoid these situations or develop new alternatives for handling them.

At the end of the first month, and at the end of each month for the first year of your freedom from cigarettes, read through the first chapter of Part I to remind yourself why you wanted to quit smoking. Then read through the other chapters to remind yourself how addicted you were to cigarettes. Then read your "good-bye" and "hello" letters again to remind yourself how you separated from your old friend, Cigarettes.

✎ *At the end of each month for a year, devote a paragraph to one of these subjects:*

1. Why am I grateful today that I quit smoking?
2. How has my life been better since I quit smoking?
3. How do people react to me now that I am a nonsmoker?
4. How do I handle stress differently now that I am a nonsmoker?
5. How has my health improved now that I am a nonsmoker?
6. What feelings do I deal with differently now that I am a non-smoker?
7. Now that I have not smoked for several months, what changes am I aware of that I did not notice before?
8. What have I used to replace cigarettes?
9. What are my attitudes about cigarettes, smoking, and smokers today?
10. How do I deal now with people who still smoke?
11. What have I learned about myself this past year?
12. What are my goals for next year?

As before, discuss what you have learned about yourself and your recovery with those you care about and those who share your experiences.

On the one-year anniversary of having quit smoking, review your daily and monthly mini-projects, and then add an anniversary letter.

Lots of folks write a Christmas letter each year to people they see and hear from only occasionally to keep them apprised of new developments in their lives. On your one-year anniversary of quitting, write out such a letter to keep Tobacco apprised of your progress. Start your letter with "Dear Tobacco, here is how I am doing and here is why I don't need you anymore." If possible, read it to the same friend you read your "Good-bye Tobacco" letter to before, or choose a new friend to share it with. If you are participating in a group, share it with the group.

All these activities—daily, monthly, and yearly—will help you maintain your abstinence, continue your recovery, increase your motivation, and reduce your risk of relapse. Relapses begin when smoking becomes possible, not when you smoke the first cigarette. The cigarette is the culmination of the relapse. These projects will give you an opportunity to "Stop the BUS" when you recognize that your relapse process has begun.

GETTING BACK WITH THE PROGRAM AFTER A RELAPSE

Read this section now and mark it. Return to it should you start smoking again.

Alcoholics accept a small medallion, called a "chip," when they join AA and express the desire to stay sober. If they relapse to drinking and then come back to an AA meeting, they exchange their "wet" chip for a "dry" one. Even though they relapsed, they still have a foundation in the program to build on. Similarly, if you relapse to smoking, you won't be starting out again from scratch; you will have learned a lot about yourself and your smoking. If you relapse, it will be because you left something undone or incomplete or you failed to take your addiction seriously enough. Getting back with the program means you will need to discover what was left undone and how you began to romance smoking again.

First, look back to see if you skipped over some of the projects in this book. Bypassing any of them puts your recovery in jeopardy. If you did skip any, complete them now.

Next, imagine that you could step out of your body and look at yourself as others see you. If you started smoking again, what advice would they give you?

✎ *Who should you call for support, advice, and encouragement?*

✎ *Which sections should you reread first?*

✎ *Which projects should you do over again?*

✎ *What other sources of help, professional or nonprofessional, should you seek out?*

Sounds like good advice.

I hope you will never have to complete this project. However, the reality is that most smokers relapse within a year of quitting. If you want to be among those who do not relapse, make this program work for you *now.* And if you do relapse, get back on track as soon as possible.

Skills of Staying Quit

Can you learn new skills? Sure you can. You have bought new tools and appliances and learned how to use them. You have moved to a new part of town or a new city and learned your way around. You have started a new job and learned how to do it. So you know you can learn new skills.

Throughout this program, you have been learning the skills of staying off cigarettes. Learning about addictions and about nicotine is helpful, but not sufficient. Learning about your dependency on nicotine is helpful, but not sufficient. Learning more about yourself is helpful, but not sufficient. You also need to learn the skills of recovery.

Someone who has never smoked might say, "What skills? Just don't smoke." You and all other addicted smokers know that it isn't quite that easy. But even after you are this far along in your journey to health, you may not recognize the skills you have been learning. This chapter will help you identify what skills you have learned and will encourage you to accept credit for having learned them.

RECOVERY SKILLS

You are learning how to stay motivated

When you first began reading this book, you may not have been sure you wanted to stick with it. There were plenty of good reasons to abandon the effort. But you managed, one way or another, to keep going. You took the motivation you already had, enhanced it, and built on it. When your motivation weakened (as everyone's does from time to time), you learned how to strengthen it. Maintaining motivation is crucial to the success of any project, so the skills you have learned here will help you in other ways too.

You are learning to develop patience

It would have been easier and far less tedious to have skipped a few of the sections in this book, but you forced yourself to be patient. From this you learned that patience has its rewards; you made progress by patiently working each project in turn. Each time you were patient, the next frustration became a little easier to handle.

You are learning to examine your behavior

You are learning how to look at what you do, say, think, and feel as another person might look at you. This is no small feat. It requires courage and vision to be able to step back and say, *Now why did I do that?* Instead of taking all your behavior for granted, you are beginning to peel back your defenses and examine your motivations. You may not always like what you see, but you are now discovering that events stop controlling you and you start controlling them.

You are learning to set goals

Many people bumble along through life, never having a very clear idea of where they are headed or why. They are tossed about by the winds of life, having little control over their course. You are learning to set goals, determine objectives, plan strategy, identify needed information, accept responsibility, and initiate action. You will get what you want out of life because you can now see where you are headed more clearly.

You are learning to think a situation through

Instead of just reacting to bad news, a stressful situation, or a conflict, you are developing the skills of contemplating an action and looking into the future to see what that action would result in. You are then deciding on current actions in light of future events. You are learning to *act,* instead of just *react.* You will make fewer bad decisions and more good ones this way.

You are learning how to evaluate options

There are usually several directions you can choose from, each of which leads somewhere different or through different territory to the same goal. If you allow yourself to remain a victim of either circumstances or the will of others, you limit your options. While this may have been acceptable to you once, you now see that your life will be fuller and richer when you are free to choose. But it adds another level of anxiety in your life: now you have a responsibility to make sensible choices. And now you won't be able to blame others for your failures, because you made the choices.

You are learning that there are always alternatives

Some may not be pleasant; some may be too costly; some may involve an unacceptable risk—but there are *always* alternatives. This book focuses on alternatives to smoking, but you can learn to identify alternatives in every area of your life. Being successful may mean choosing a painful or difficult alternative today in order to reach your goal tomorrow. You have learned how to turn down a cigarette (even though you may have wanted one) because you had a goal in mind. Now you can apply this skill to other areas of your life.

You are learning to take responsibility

It's not your fault that you became addicted to cigarettes—you certainly didn't plan to become addicted when you started smoking. You probably would never have started smoking if it hadn't been for peer pressure or the example of your parents or other role models who smoked. So you could blame someone else for your dependence on cigarettes—others have. But now you are learning how to take responsibility for your own actions, your own life, and your own future. You have no need to blame others for what has happened to you. Once you accept this responsibility, you discover a tremendous sense of relief and freedom because you now have more control of your destiny. You have learned that when you make others responsible for your problems, they will want credit for your successes. When you accept responsibility for your own life, you gain mastery over your future.

You are learning to have the courage to face things about yourself that you don't like

Even more important, you are learning to search for ways to improve. You have done most of this work on your own. You are discovering that you have more courage to deal with your shortcomings than you thought you had.

You are learning that you won't get anything accomplished unless you begin now

The Chinese philosopher Lao-tzu said, "A journey of a thousand miles begins with a single step." You were reluctant to enter this program in the first place, and there were some projects you balked at completing. But you discovered that once you ventured forth, ideas began to form in your head and the words began to flow. You began, and now you have accomplished something worthwhile. You will approach the next challenge in your life with the certain knowledge that you can achieve your goals if you start now.

You are learning to be more sensitive to the needs of others

In group sessions and in Nicotine Anonymous meetings, you are being supportive of other smokers who are trying to quit. Instead of mocking them if they stumble, you are encouraging them to continue. Bill Wilson, the cofounder of Alcoholics Anonymous, discovered that he could only stay sober by helping others try to stay sober; you, too, are discovering that supporting others who are trying to quit helps you to stay quit.

You are learning how to connect with others

When you first opened this book, you may have looked around at other smokers and focused on the differences between you and them. *Well, I never burned a hole in a suit!* you might have thought after reading one of the vignettes in Part I or II. But lately, you are noticing the similarities between you and other smokers instead of the differences. You are becoming willing to be a part of a new community—a community of recovering nonsmokers who choose not to smoke, one day at a time.

You are learning to listen to others

Sometimes others actually have something worthwhile to say—but you may not have always paid attention before. Through looking at the needs of others, through sharing your experiences with a group, and through seeing yourself as a member of a community, you have developed a greater ability to accept what others have to say. You are putting this little prayer into action:

Lord, fill my mouth with useful stuff
But hush me when I've said enough.

You are learning to look to the future

You are beginning to realize that as much as you might want to, you cannot change the past, but you can make a better future for yourself and those you care about. When you were a smoker, you hardly gave a thought to the way your smoking intruded on others. Now that you have quit, you may become acutely aware of the stench of stale cigarette smoke, of the cloud hanging over groups of smokers, and of the mess created by butts, ashes, and ashtrays. You may feel your own space being intruded on by smokers—and you may be chagrined when you realize what you looked like when you smoked every day. You might want to rewrite the past, but today you know that instead of dwelling on past errors, you can invest your energies in creating a better future.

You are learning to think positively

Instead of dwelling on failures and weaknesses, you are beginning to concentrate on successes and strengths. When you identify a failure, you are learning to reset it as a new goal, not obsess about it as a permanent liability. Recognizing your considerable achievements and good qualities increases your self-esteem, making you even more likely to accept a new challenge (and making you more likely to succeed at it).

You are learning that you are a good person

Your self-esteem is higher and your self-confidence is greater. You like yourself better and you are finding that you can like other people too.

You are learning that you don't have to hide

In the past, you may have used cigarettes to hide behind. When asked a threatening question, you could pause—grope for your pack, extract a cigarette, snap your lighter, inhale deeply, exhale profoundly—and then say, "Excuse me, but what was that question again?" When placed in an exposed or uncomfortably public position (especially if you had a shy streak you kept hidden), the cigarette became a defensive weapon, and the cloud you exhaled was a real "smoke screen." It kept you safely hidden from others; they couldn't see who you were or how insecure you felt. But now you are learning to be honest with these feelings and honest with yourself, and your need to hide has left.

You are learning to make amends

There have been many whom you have hurt in some way with your smoking. You are becoming more aware of some of these incidents, and you may have carried your guilt around with you like an unwieldy backpack. Making amends to these people frees you from the guilt and shame, replacing it with a feeling of relief. As your recovery progresses, you will complete this process.

You are learning to trust others

You may never have been part of a group process before, so joining a group and attending Nicotine Anonymous meetings have been new experiences. You may be a very private person, unused to discussing personal feelings with others. You may be an outgoing person with lots of friends, but what you usually share with them may be superficial. Participating in a group, sharing something of yourself, receiving feedback from others, and learning to trust the group may have been one of your most positive experiences in recovery.

You are learning to set priorities in your life

Many of the things you thought were crucial turned out not to be. You may have been hanging on to some old stuff for fear of failure. Now you can set sensible and realistic priorities in your life. The things you do are not all of equal importance. Some of your goals may have been misguided, and maintaining them was like carrying around excess baggage that weighed you down. Setting new priorities means you can chuck the excess baggage and pay attention to what is most important.

You are learning to be assertive

You are learning how to get your needs met without infringing on the rights of others. You are standing up for your right to have clean air to breathe. There is a right way and a wrong way to keep your space clean, and you are developing the skills of doing it the right way.

You are learning to take life *one day at a time*

If need be, you can take life one hour or one minute at a time. When stresses mount and you imagine that a cigarette would certainly taste good, you are learning how to pause, step back, and not smoke just yet. You don't have to plan to be a nonsmoker forever—you need only be a nonsmoker *today.* Tomorrow you can renew the pledge. Taking it one day at a time works for staying smoke-free just as well as it works for staying drug-free and sober. You will also discover how well it works in dealing with other stresses in your life.

You are learning how to plan to succeed instead of setting yourself up for failure

Your self-defeating behaviors have all too often kept you from achieving what you were capable of achieving. This time, you set out to succeed, and you are succeeding.

You are learning to identify your feelings

Many people find it difficult to identify their feelings, so at first you may not have even seen this difficulty as a problem. After all, cigarette smoking isn't alcoholism or heroin addiction! You could see how alcoholics and addicts ought to work on this, but not smokers. Then you learned how easy it is to mislabel feelings and how people suffer from not being able to understand what they feel. Now you are working on being honest with your feelings. Now you can see how you have used cigarettes to help you deal with shyness, loneliness, anger, frustration, confusion, grief, rejection, resentment, fear, anxiety, embarrassment, and a host of other feelings.

You are becoming a more spiritual person

As you faced your smoking addiction and learned more about yourself, your insight improved and your relationships with others took on new meanings. You now feel more connected with others than you did. You are becoming a better person.

You are learning how to take time for yourself

You may have sacrificed so much for others in the past that you did not give much attention to your own needs. This program has required a great deal of your time and effort—and you invested it in yourself. This was something you did by yourself and for yourself. And you deserve everything you have accomplished.

You are learning about the incredible power of addictions

Of course, there was a time when you didn't think that you were addicted. But now you know that cigarettes are addicting and that you are addicted. And what's more, you are coming to accept it. This discovery will change your life. What seemed disastrous a few chapters ago now seems part of life. Be proud of yourself for having faced the fact that tobacco is addicting and that you are addicted to it.

About 15 percent of the people who read this book are learning that they are addicted to another chemical besides tobacco. If you are one of these people, you are developing *the courage to face another addiction.* Most of what this book says about nicotine addiction is equally true for alcohol addiction, cocaine addiction, sedative addiction, and all the other drug addictions. Much of it is also true for compulsive behaviors with addictive characteristics, such as anorexia/bulimia syndromes, compulsive overeating, compulsive sexuality, and compulsive gambling. If the courage you have shown in facing nicotine addiction helps you face other addictions and compulsions, the time you invested in this program will have been worthwhile.

You are learning to be satisfied with what you have accomplished

Your goal is progress, not perfection. Your desire to smoke may never go away completely—but so what? You may have a secret desire to go skydiving, but you probably won't actually try it. You may harbor hopes of joining a Tibetan monastery, but the chances are you won't ever go. You may have thought about standing up in the management meeting and punching the boss in the face, but you know you won't do it. So you can look at your continuing desire for a cigarette as simply one more fantasy you will never act on. And as you become satisfied with your progress in recovery, you can learn to become satisfied with your progress in other areas.

You are learning to appreciate your progress, however gradual it might be

You don't need to be perfect. If it took you longer to quit than it took someone else, so what? You know that *staying* quit is more important than *when* you quit. You may have relapsed and started smoking again. You can now accept that. You have learned that addictions are chronic diseases, characterized by relapses and remissions. Your relapse only signaled that more remained to be done; it did not mean failure.

Yes, you should be pleased with your progress. Too often, we only look ahead to where we need to go and forget to look behind to see how far we've come. Turn around now, scan that horizon, and see how much progress you've already made.

✎ *In your journal, list some of the skills you now have to help you stay quit.*

Be proud of all your newly learned skills. Keep practicing them and adding to them, and they will serve you well in the future.

– 8 –

Imagination

Imagination is the most powerful force ever discovered. Your imagination can travel where your body never will. In your imagination, you can complete what your body is barely able to begin. You can imagine experiences you will never be able to have, except in your imagination.

Like other powerful forces, such as fire or wind, imagination is capable of causing great good or great harm. Fire can warm your home or burn it down; wind can speed your ship along or capsize it. So, too, can your imagination motivate you or destroy you.

Imagination helps you when you think about the person you would like to be, the goals you want to attain, and the changes you want to make. You can imagine a calm scene and become calmer. You can imagine how you might solve a particular problem and become better equipped to actually solve it. You can imagine becoming a non-smoker and then become one.

Imagination becomes your foe when, after having stayed off cigarettes for some time, you begin to dream about the pleasures of smoking again. Your romance with cigarettes may again begin to gain power over you. You imagine that you might be able to control your smoking this time, though you never could before. In your fantasies, this time will be different.

There is no earthly force to stop that runaway imagination. Threats won't help. Pleading won't help. Logic won't help. None of these forces are powerful enough.

The popular motivational speaker Zig Ziglar says that there is only *one* force powerful enough to do battle with imagination, and it is . . .

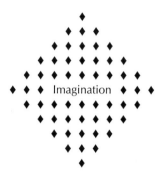

The way to halt your rekindled romance with cigarettes is to use your imagination again.

Relapses occur in the course of any addictive disease, and your cigarette dependence is no exception. One goal in recovery is to prevent relapse. How will you know if a relapse is imminent? Look at what is in your imagination.

- Are you starting to fantasize about smoking again?
- Are you beginning to imagine what it would be like to smoke again?
- Are you again thinking about how much you enjoyed smoking?
- Are you remembering how nice it was to have a cigarette with a cup of coffee or after a meal?
- Do you think about smoking when you smell someone else's cigarette or see someone else light up?
- Do you discover that you are holding a pen or a straw between your fingers the way you used to hold a cigarette?
- Have you caught yourself pretending to smoke using a pen, a pencil, a straw, or a coffee stir stick?
- As you drift off to sleep, do you think about the cigarette you used to smoke before retiring for the night?
- As the sun sets, do you long for the days when you relaxed with a cigarette, a cigar, or a pipe at sunset?

If you are doing any of these things, you are romancing cigarettes.

Your imagination is leading you down the primrose path to relapse.

If you discover that you are romancing your cigarettes again, step back and pause and observe the power and cunning of this adversary, your smoking dependence. Through your imagination, smoking has again attempted to entice you back into its addictive clutches.

Fight back! Use the healthy side of your imagination. Before you smoke your next cigarette, thoroughly think through your last cigarette.

- What was it like to be dependent on cigarettes?
- Didn't I put out considerable effort to quit?
- When I quit, how did I feel about smoking?
- If I smoke this cigarette, will I stop when it's finished?
- If I smoke this entire pack, what will I feel like tomorrow?
- If I show up smoking tomorrow, what excuse will I use? Will anyone believe it?
- How embarrassed am I willing to be in order to smoke today?
- Is this just temporary insanity that will soon pass?
- Can I delay smoking this cigarette for five minutes, or one minute, or half a minute?
- If I do smoke this cigarette, how will I feel about myself?
- If I don't smoke this cigarette, how will I feel about myself?
- Is this cigarette worth it? Is it *really* worth it?

Imagine yourself putting away the pack of cigarettes, and not smoking—just for five minutes. Imagine the strength you will need to do that. Imagine how you will feel after you succeed at not smoking today. Imagine how proud of yourself you will be.

Imagine yourself smoking. Imagine having to make up all sorts of excuses for why you smoked. Imagine explaining to your co-workers, your family, and your friends why you went back to smoking. Imagine explaining it to yourself in the mirror tomorrow morning. If your heart and lungs could speak, what would they say? Imagine trying to justify smoking to them.

Now imagine *not* having to make those excuses.

Imagine being the person you really want to be. Does that person smoke? Imagine having the qualities you most want to have. Is a person with those admirable qualities controlled by an addicting chemical?

Make your imagination your ally. It can be a good one.

✎ *In your journal, list ways you can use your imagination to help you.*

– 9 –

Making Amends

You have made many changes in your life since you started this program; not smoking is only one of them. Aren't you impressed with your personal growth? Ridding yourself of any remaining guilt about smoking will help free you to continue this growth.

Some guilt can be useful. When you feel guilty, it means you have done something contrary to your own moral values. Therefore, your sense of guilt reminds you that you need to make improvements. Too much guilt, however, puts your mind in turmoil and holds you back. You then have a choice: you can live with this turmoil, or you can try to resolve it. If you choose to live with it, you may need to use chemicals or dysfunctional behavior (gambling, arguing, sex, eating, or isolating) to tolerate the conflict. If you decide to resolve it, you have two choices: you can change your behavior, or you can decide that the things you did were perfectly acceptable.

Knowing what you know now about yourself and your life, what will be your choice?

In the past when you felt guilty about something you said or how you treated someone, you may have used nicotine to suppress the uncomfortable feelings. Now you are choosing not to use nicotine. Of course, you could drink alcohol or take Valium instead, or take refuge in compulsive sexuality or seething resentments. Alternatively, you could continue to carry the guilt around with you, forever limiting your potential and keeping you unhappy.

Another choice would be to alleviate your guilty feelings by making amends.

By now, you've accepted your cigarette addiction and have dealt with many of your unhealthy behaviors. You haven't smoked in some time and you have developed a relapse prevention plan. You've thought about the changes you've made and have recognized your progress. Now it's time to examine the things you've done that you regret and the situations you wish you'd handled differently.

Perhaps you're not aware that you have guilty feelings about your smoking.

Were you reluctant at first to tell people you were trying to quit smoking? If so, why do you suppose that was? Was it out of fear of being rejected, or of offending someone, or of disappointing the people who care about you? Surely, everyone you've told about your efforts to quit has been supportive. They have been glad to hear you are improving your health, increasing your longevity, and making your environment more pleasant. So why were you hesitant to tell people you were quitting?

Perhaps it was from fear of failure:

If I don't tell anyone I'm quitting, then I won't have to feel like a failure if I can't quit.

Perhaps it was because you felt a little foolish:

I know I should have quit long ago; if I don't make a big deal out of it, maybe no one will notice and they'll assume I quit a long time ago.

Perhaps it was because you felt embarrassed:

I've told people so many times that I was going to quit—I can't play that old song again; no one will listen.

You may still harbor a fear of failure, feel a little foolish for having smoked so long, and be embarrassed at not having quit sooner. These are examples of how feelings of guilt can be labeled as something else. "Guilt" simply means that you have conflicting feelings because you did something you think you should not have done.

You may also try to talk yourself out of feeling guilty by blaming your behavior on various "causes":

- Stupidity . . .
  I can't believe I smoked all those years—I was an idiot to ever start smoking, and I should have quit long ago.
- Ignorance . . .
  When I started smoking, no one knew it caused cancer.
- Avoiding rejection . . .
  I have never really enjoyed smoking. I only smoked to be part of the crowd and to be accepted.
- Clumsiness . . .
  I'm sorry about your coffee table. I'm such a klutz. Have it refinished and send me the bill.
- Age . . .
  When I was your age, we didn't have Nintendo and malls. Smoking was what we did for fun.
- Rebelliousness . . .
  If my parents hadn't been so adamant against my smoking, I don't think I ever would have started. I only picked it up because it made them mad.
- The tobacco companies . . .
  Cigarette ads make smoking seem so glamorous. That's why I started smoking.
- Someone else . . .
  I never smoked until I got married. I don't think I ever would have smoked if I had married a nonsmoker.

Having learned a great deal about smoking and nicotine by reading this book, you recognize today that you weren't smoking because you were stupid, ignorant, lonely, clumsy, youthful, rebellious, gullible, or easily corrupted. You may have *started* smoking for one of these reasons, but you continued to smoke because you became addicted to cigarettes, and when you wanted to stop, you discovered that you could not. You *feel* guilty about your behavior, but you protect your feelings by intellectualizing them and convincing yourself that you just made a mistake or that someone else was to blame.

Failure to deal with these feelings puts you at risk of relapse. As much as you would like to skip the rest of this chapter, you owe it to yourself to continue.

You might take the position that you have no guilt because (a) your behavior was preordained, (b) everyone is responsible for his or her own feelings, or (c) things always work out the way they are supposed to. Even if you believe you are guilt-free, just consider the possibility that a kernel of guilt remains in your mind and read through the rest of this chapter anyway.

LETTING GO OF THE GUILT

After quitting, most smokers harbor guilty feelings over things they've done and people they've hurt because of their smoking. Recovering smokers have different responses to these feelings:

- Some become defensive when their old behaviors are mentioned.
- Some become aggressive nonsmokers, pulling cigarettes from the lips of smokers, dramatically fanning away tobacco smoke, or loudly telling a smoker to stop smoking.
- Some become passionate defenders of nonsmokers' rights.
- Some become equally passionate defenders of *smokers'* rights.
- Some become silly, sarcastic, or argumentative when smoking is mentioned.
- Some become unnecessarily demonstrative about how they have quit smoking but others have not.

✎ *What kind of nonsmoker do you want to be?*

If you want to be comfortable with your recovery, you must deal with any feelings of guilt or resentment that remain within you.

You may have harmed many people because of your smoking, some knowingly and some unknowingly, most inadvertently. You may have caused discomfort to any number of travelers, diners, sports fans, or friends by clouding up the air they were breathing. You may have burnt a hole in someone else's clothing, furniture, carpet, or car seats. You may have contributed to someone's asthma, allergy attack, or sinus headache without even being aware of it. And only now that you are working on changing your life and reordering your priorities can you begin to notice all this.

When you tell people that you are quitting, you leave yourself open to the possibility that they will remind you of many more ways in which your smoking imposed on others. When people are convinced you will stay quit, they may tell you more than you want to hear about the effects your smoking had on those around you. So this takes courage.

- "Boy, I'm sure glad to hear you're quitting! Maybe now it'll be safe to recover the sofa in the den!"
  Gee, I don't recall damaging the sofa.

- "How wonderful that you've quit. I can already tell by the difference in how your breath smells!"
  What? You mean my breath smelled that bad?

- "I could tell you quit, actually; you didn't even need to tell me, because those crow's-feet around your eyes are fading away."
  Crow's-feet? Me?

You see, the people who really care about you noticed that you smoked a lot, and they were aware of its impact on you. They were hoping that you would quit smoking. Now they are happy that you have quit. They may be skeptical of your ability to stay quit and may not mention these past events or their remaining resentments for a while. But eventually you can expect to hear about how your smoking affected others. Will you be ready for it? Will you have developed a mechanism for dealing with guilt so that when new information comes to light, you will be able to deal with it?

There is a way to do this. It's called "making amends."

There is nothing new or original about making amends. Catholics go to confession to get absolved from their sins. Jews ask the forgiveness of other people and God during the High Holy Days. Members of Alcoholics Anonymous take an Eighth Step: "Made a list of all persons we had harmed, and became willing to make amends to them all," and a Ninth Step: "Made direct amends to such people wherever possible, except when to do so would injure them or others." These are all ways of becoming honest with oneself and letting go of feelings of guilt.

Try to find a way of relieving guilt that works for you. Many recovering smokers have been successful by making amends the way it's done in Alcoholics Anonymous. This will be the focus of the remainder of this chapter.

LISTING AMENDS THAT NEED TO BE MADE

✎ *What persons, places, or things have been harmed by your smoking? Are there people you have imposed on, situations you have affected, or property you have damaged by smoking? Compose a thorough list.*

People I have harmed in some way by my smoking:
- ❑ spouse
- ❑ children
- ❑ parents
- ❑ relatives
- ❑ neighbors
- ❑ co-workers
- ❑ clerks
- ❑ carpool buddies
- ❑ customers
- ❑ dentist
- ❑ friends (and ex-friends)
- ❑ someone on an elevator
- ❑ restaurant patrons
- ❑ the guy in the next seat
- ❑ bridge partner

How I have damaged property with my smoking:
- ❑ I have burned holes or marks in my furniture.
- ❑ I have burned holes in my neighbors' furniture.
- ❑ I have spilled ashes on the living room carpet.
- ❑ I have dropped my cigarette on the bedspread and burned it.
- ❑ I have ruined clothing by dropping hot ashes on it.
- ❑ I have burned my desk at work with my cigarettes.
- ❑ I have ruined my car seats by dropping hot ashes on them.
- ❑ I have stained my teeth or dentures so badly I can't get the stains out.

Relationships I have affected by my smoking:

- ❏ the relationship with my parents
- ❏ the relationship with my friends
- ❏ the relationship with my children
- ❏ the relationship with my old friends
- ❏ the relationship with my spouse
- ❏ the relationship with my co-workers
- ❏ the relationship with my relatives
- ❏ the relationship with my doctor
- ❏ the relationships that began but were terminated because I smoked

List as many ways as you can think of in which these people, things, and relationships were affected by your smoking. Over the week or two that it will take you to complete this list, you are likely to discover many more instances than you are aware of today.

In working this project, you will truly be facing your smoking addiction. And until you have worked it, you will still be hiding from the impact smoking has had on your life.

This section comes at the end of this book because it is only after having done a significant amount of work that you can be expected to face this task. It requires a great deal of courage. The longer your list becomes, the less you are going to want to work on it. But this crucial project will help free you from guilt and help you get on with your life as a nonsmoker.

Eventually, your list will be as complete as you can make it.

You will have faced the fact that you owe amends to many people because of your smoking. Some of these people will no longer be part of your life and recalling your relationship with them may cause you much sadness.

Your list may be quite long, making you feel even more guilty than you did before, when you were able to avoid reality. At this point, you may wish to forget the whole thing. If you begin to think this way, just remember how far you have come. Yes, this work may be strenuous and even embarrassing, but the personal rewards will be great.

Your next challenge is to actually make these amends.

MAKING AMENDS

Are you ready to move on to making amends? There may be some you are prepared to make now and some you need to reserve for another time. You may be able to make partial amends to some people now and can plan to complete this project in the future.

These are normal feelings. Making amends can be painful. You may need to explore your feelings for a while before you are ready. Some recovering smokers find that working individually with a therapist is helpful; others turn to group therapy or to Nicotine Anonymous for support and advice.

One at a time, begin making amends to all the people on your list, except those who would be hurt or injured in some way. Let them know that you have quit smoking and that part of your motivation to quit and stay quit comes from remembering what your smoking did to them. Tell them you are sorry for your insensitivity and that you now realize that you were addicted to cigarettes. Apologize for any harm you might have caused because of your smoking.

Asking forgiveness and making things right can be upsetting and awkward. You may try to find reasons for putting off this project, and you may succeed in doing so—for a day, a week, a month, or longer.

When recovering alcoholics in Alcoholics Anonymous balk at a point like this, their sponsors ask, "Are you willing to go to any lengths to get sober and stay sober?" Ask yourself the same question: *Am I willing to go to any lengths to quit and stay quit? How badly do I want to recover?* Painful though this process may be, making amends will help you reach your goals.

You can make your amends in a letter, on the phone, or in person. You can do it alone or with others. Keep a record of the amends you have made and what you learned from the experience. Each time you will discover more about yourself and your relationships with others.

When you set out to make amends with someone, take it seriously, and be sure the person you are apologizing to understands how important this is to you. Practicing often helps; you might try role-playing the situation with a therapist or a trusted friend or in a group. Will this be stressful? Sure. But the experiences of thousands of recovering people suggest that it is worth the effort. Writing your "Good-bye Tobacco" letter was difficult but rewarding. Making amends will be too.

Making amends can help reestablish a broken relationship or heal a damaged one. It can also endanger a tenuous relationship. The Chinese word for *crisis* can be used to illustrate this situation:

Together, these two characters (pronounced "wei gi") form the word for *crisis.* The upper character means "danger"; the lower, "opportunity." Thus, every crisis brings together elements of danger and opportunity. Making amends combines both elements. Will you focus only on the danger, or will you also see the opportunity?

Begin with one amend that you feel confident will not be a struggle. Succeeding with one crisis will give you confidence to meet the next one. One by one, accept the challenge and make the amends on your list.

As the months and years pass, you will inevitably recognize other amends to be made. But by then you will feel more comfortable in your recovery, and completing your amends will become much easier.

Clean from cigarettes, and released from guilt over having smoked so many of them, you are ready for further personal growth. The chapter ahead will help you plan for it.

✎ *On a separate sheet of paper, write about the amends you have made and what you have learned by making them.*

– 10 –

A Look at Your Success and Setting Goals for the Future

Success. Doesn't that have a nice ring to it?

You've done well. Now is the time to savor the real "taste of success" before moving on to other challenges.

All too often, people keep looking forward, searching the horizon for the path ahead, straining to see how much farther they have to go. They may despair when they realize how far away their goal lies. Occasionally, they need to look back over their shoulder and compare where they are with where they were.

You probably began this program simply to stop smoking. But in the process you have no doubt discovered a great deal about yourself. Your cigarettes were intimately involved in every area of your life. So you have accomplished much more than you thought you would—you have not only stopped smoking, you have also become a better person.

Turn around for a minute and check out how far you have come. When you started this program, did you think you would get this far? Did you think you would succeed?

✎ My greatest accomplishments in this program have been . . .

Take pride in your success. There have been few things you have ever done for which you deserve more praise and recognition than quitting smoking.

Be proud of your success, and let it be a springboard to more successes in your life. Having accomplished this challenge (which you once thought impossible), you will find that other challenges will seem less imposing.

What exactly have you done?

- You have looked at why you needed to stop smoking.
- You have faced and accepted the addictive nature of your smoking.
- You have examined your dependent behaviors.
- You have learned that cigarettes were manipulating your life.
- You have decided to be a positive thinker.
- You have chosen methods other than smoking to relieve stress.
- You have looked at your life as a sequence of events over which you have influence and have decided not to remain a victim.
- You have accepted that you would miss cigarettes but that the benefits of not smoking were worth it.
- You have learned how to look at your attitudes and your behavior in new ways.
- You have learned that you can change your attitudes and behavior.
- You became ready to give up smoking in spite of its pleasures.
- You sought the help of others to accomplish this and gave the same help to others who needed it.
- You made a plan to smoke your last cigarette and carried it out.
- You have found new techniques for controlling anxiety and stress.
- You have discovered you could free yourself from guilt by honestly expressing your feelings.
- You have developed a solid plan to avoid relapse.
- You have made amends to those you have harmed by your smoking.
- You have learned how to stay quit.

Congratulations. You did it.

Attitudes about Smoking III

Have your attitudes about cigarettes, smoking, smokers, and the future changed since you finished Part II in this book?

1. What is your attitude about cigarettes *today?* Here are some examples:

   - Tobacco farmers must learn to grow something else and tobacco workers must be retrained. The reality is that Americans are quitting smoking, and the economies of North Carolina and Kentucky must adapt.
   - If some people want to kill themselves by smoking, that's their business. I hope I never smoke again.
   - Cigarettes are addicting. It's a shame that something can't be done to prevent kids from starting to smoke.

✎ My attitude . . .

2. What is your attitude about smoking *today?* Here are some examples:

   - My head tells me smoking is dumb, but my emotions tell me I wish I could smoke again.
   - Smoking is a disgusting habit and a compulsive addiction. I can understand why it's so hard for people to quit.
   - I understand now that I am a nicotine and tobacco addict. Smoking is just not something I can do anymore.

✎ My attitude . . .

3. What is your attitude about smokers *today?* Here are some examples:

- I tend to be a little too aggressive toward smokers. I never hesitate to tell people to put out their cigarettes.
- I think that smokers who kick the habit should get more recognition. And their insurance should pick up the tab for their smoking cessation treatment.
- They'd all be a lot better off if they quit.

✎ My attitude . . .

4. What is your attitude about the future *today?* Here are some examples:

- I know what you're getting at. Just because I quit smoking does not mean everything else is going to fall into place. Becoming a nonsmoker sure isn't going to get me a better job or a raise.
- I'm really glad I quit smoking. I've never done anything quite like this program before. Maybe it will help me somehow in the future.
- I feel a lot healthier than I did when I was smoking. I've got a pretty good outlook on the future, I think. I'd like to do something to help other smokers quit. As a matter of fact, I've been thinking about starting my own smoking clinic.

✎ My attitude . . .

Now that you have explored your attitudes about cigarettes, smoking, smokers, and the future on three occasions, you might be interested in going back to the "attitudes" chapters in Parts I and II (pages 61–66 and pages 147–148) to see how your attitudes have changed.

– 12 –

Questions and Answers III

I'm still irritable and it's been three months since I quit smoking. When will I get better?

You are already better. Congratulations on not smoking for three months. Your body and your mind are already healing.

Irritability is a normal *subacute* withdrawal symptom. *Subacute* means it lasts longer than an *acute* symptom, which occurs immediately after you quit and goes away in a week or so (like panicking whenever you see someone smoking or feeling like punching out people you have never met before). Subacute symptoms will resolve in time. *Chronic* symptoms, on the other hand, are ones that may never go away (like wanting a cigarette after having sex or being distracted by the tobacco display in a store).

Subacute symptoms, such as unconsciously touching the pocket where you used to carry cigarettes, feeling nervous in situations in which you used to smoke, and having frightening dreams or the irritability you mentioned, will go away eventually. Every person is a little different. Some people never have such symptoms at all, or will have them for only a few days. Others are bothered by them for a year. No one can say when yours will dissipate.

Some symptoms, frankly, may never go away. The satisfaction of toying with a cigarette-shaped object (like a stir stick or a pencil), wanting a cigarette after a frightening experience (like an automobile accident or after receiving bad news), or the nagging thought that "maybe I can smoke just one"—these symptoms and many others may be with you as long as you live. I haven't smoked a pipe in many years, yet I can still detect the aroma of Captain Black tobacco five miles away. I'm not going to smoke, but I'm aware that I am still attracted to the smell.

If I stay off cigarettes for a year, can I start smoking a pipe?

If you start smoking a pipe, you will absorb almost as much nicotine as you did from your cigarettes, even if you do not inhale the smoke. Pipe and cigar smoke is alkaline, meaning the nicotine is not ionized and is therefore easily absorbed across the tissues of the mouth, tongue, and throat. Since cigarette smoke is acidic, the nicotine in it is ionized and cannot be absorbed well from the mouth—though it is absorbed very well from the lungs.

Pipe and cigar smokers who do not inhale have a somewhat increased incidence of lung cancer over nonsmokers, but have an enormously increased incidence of cancers of the mouth, tongue, and related structures. Those who do inhale are probably at the same risk for all cancers as cigarette smokers.

Recovering alcoholics frequently start using a chemical other than alcohol in the hope that they can use it "in control." They may use Valium or marijuana in this way. However, they usually return to using alcohol, their "drug of choice," and usually the specific type and brand they used before. Some who previously drank only whiskey or vodka try to drink in control by switching to beer, but soon find themselves drinking beer out of control or going back to whiskey or vodka. The alcohol is the same, regardless of which alcoholic beverage it comes in: a twelve-ounce can of beer, a jigger of whiskey, and a four-ounce glass of table wine all contain about the same amount of alcohol.

What can you learn from that? If you start smoking a pipe, it may start out as an intermittent pastime, but it will soon become a dependency as intense as your previous one on cigarettes. The nicotine is the same, regardless of which form the tobacco comes in. There is nicotine in pipe tobacco, cigar tobacco, cigarette tobacco, snuff tobacco, chewing tobacco, Nicorette gum, and the nicotine skin patch. The form of delivery is different, but the nicotine is the same. If you were dependent on nicotine before, you will become so again.

And you will most likely start smoking cigarettes again, because they did things for you that the pipe will not do.

If you want to maintain your abstinence and continue your recovery, do not start smoking a pipe.

What can I do to help other smokers quit?

An admirable desire. Thousands of recovering smokers have contributed to your recovery, most of whom you have never known. The social changes that made it possible for you to quit would not have occurred had not thousands of people lobbied for clean air on airplanes, clean air in restaurants, and clean air at work.

On a more personal level, recovering smokers you do know probably helped you through some of your more difficult moments. They may have shared their experience, strength, and hope with you, telling you their stories and encouraging your progress. I sincerely hope that this book has helped you; I wrote it with the encouragement and contributions of hundreds of smokers who were patients and friends of mine.

The best place to help other smokers make progress is in Nicotine Anonymous. A few Nicotine Anonymous meetings are held in every major city, with more starting all the time. Participate in one on a regular basis, give it some leadership, and help out newcomers. Or start a new meeting in an underserved area or on a different day or at a different time. The central office of Nicotine Anonymous will offer you direction. You can reach it at the following address:

Nicotine Anonymous World Services
Box 591777
San Francisco, CA 94159-1777
Telephone (415) 750-0328

If you are a mental health or an addiction treatment professional, you might consider putting together a treatment group after you have had two years or more of abstinence and quality recovery. I would not recommend working professionally in this area any earlier than that. For one thing, it could be too stressful for you; for another, you really need to allow yourself time to integrate the changes you have made. If you want to work in this field, write to me; I will be glad to help you learn the techniques of leading such groups. (My address is listed near the end of this chapter.) Professional books on nicotine dependence treatment are now starting to be published. In addition, the publisher of this book publishes other titles on nicotine dependence that can help you.

On another level, you can be an advocate for further social and political changes to make our nation and its people smoke-free. You could talk about your experiences at a school, at your church, or among your friends; you can support progressive legislation that encourages medical and scientific research into the treatment of nicotine dependence, alternative crops for tobacco farmers, and restrictions on tobacco availability to minors. You can make your voice heard.

I suggest that you *not* become a tobacco vigilante, pulling cigarettes out of people's mouths, blowing out their matches, pompously fanning their smoke away, and otherwise making yourself a general nuisance. These actions do not advance the cause of nicotine recovery and probably do not help smokers become more willing to quit.

What is Nicotine Anonymous and how does it differ from group therapy for smoking cessation?

Nicotine Anonymous is a voluntary organization, a fellowship of men and women who use the Twelve Step principles of Alcoholics Anonymous to recover from dependence on smoking and nicotine. It collects no dues or fees and relies on contributions from members for support. It is not a treatment program; it is a fellowship of recovery. Everyone in Nicotine Anonymous is equal; no one has all the answers. Everyone shares at meetings. Everyone is striving to improve his or her recovery.

The techniques described in this book are derived from the recovery principle of Alcoholics Anonymous—accepting one's powerlessness over nicotine, learning a new way of life, and connecting with others. When this book is used as the basis of a group therapy treatment program led by a professionally trained group leader, it becomes part of recovery-oriented treatment, which is much different from a Nicotine Anonymous meeting. In the treatment setting, the group leader is *expected* to know the answers and is not expected to share personal experiences. Group members pay to attend and the leaders receive payment for their professional time.

The goal of all Twelve Step programs is abstinence through working a spiritual program based on the Steps. The goal of therapy is to discover the truth about one's life. These goals are not mutually exclusive and may be compatible, but they are different.

I've quit smoking, but my husband still smokes. What should I do?

Several studies show that when one partner quits and the other does not, the one who quits usually relapses. Your chances of staying quit are quite small as long as your husband still smokes.

Having put this much effort into quitting, you probably do not want to accept near-certain relapse. If your husband is willing to consider quitting—even just a little—encourage him. If you have been open and honest with him while you were working this program, he has some knowledge of what you have accomplished. Perhaps he would be willing to follow in your footsteps.

There is a difference, however, between *encouraging* someone to quit and making a nuisance of yourself. Snide or arrogant comments never help; neither does spraying room deodorizer all over the house, coughing dramatically, or hiding the ashtrays. If you want to help yourself *and* your partner, make an effort to communicate, not just to confront.

It will help if you know what kind of a person your partner is.

Some people are logical but cannot recognize their own feelings or those of others. They make decisions based on what makes sense. Approach these people with information about smoking and health, emphasizing how prudent it is to quit smoking. You can share how quitting has already paid you dividends.

Other people respond primarily on the basis of personal values. Their decisions center on what they believe to be worthwhile in life. Tell these people how important they are to you and how it hurts you to see them abusing themselves with smoke every day.

Some people are very competitive and respond to a challenge; others are more self-motivated. Some want to tell everyone about their quitting; others want to maintain their privacy. The key to success is to help your partner in ways he or she can accept.

If your partner is not interested in quitting after you have made significant efforts, you must protect yourself. Environmental tobacco smoke is a major cause of illness and increases your risk of relapse. You are within your rights to keep your home smoke-free. Ask your partner (and any smoking guests) to smoke outside. Removing the social and recreational aspects of smoking makes it much less attractive and thus may encourage your partner to quit.

I'm afraid that I'm going to gain a lot of weight now that I have quit smoking. What should I do?

Smoking two packs of cigarettes a day will raise your metabolic rate about 10 percent—about 5 percent when you are sedentary and about 12 percent when you are moderately active. This is due to the stimulant effect of nicotine.

After you quit smoking, your system slows down, and your need for energy drops. Food equals energy, so your need for food drops. However, many smokers start nibbling after they quit. If you substitute M & M's for cigarettes, I guarantee you will gain weight, and lots of it. Even if you eat exactly as you did before you quit, you may still gain some weight.

There is a solution, though. Now that you are no longer smoking, your endurance is better and your lungs are healthier. That means you will be able to exercise more frequently and more vigorously for longer periods of time. Twenty minutes each day of brisk walking will compensate for the change in your metabolic rate, and it will be beneficial to your heart, lungs, and muscles as well.

I just discovered that my sixteen-year-old has started smoking. What should I do?

Tell your child about your own recovery from nicotine and smoking dependence—not in an arrogant or overbearing way, but personally and sensitively. Tell your child that you understand how a teenager can become seduced into smoking, what with the peer pressure, the cigarette ads, and the cheap "high" cigarettes provide. Discuss how you started smoking, how you discovered you couldn't quit, and how you have now succeeded.

I consider it unwise to make "compromises," such as smoking at home, smoking only on weekends, approving certain brands, or buying cigarettes for kids. Teenagers flout rules anyway, and setting up certain limitations on smoking invites them to try to get away with more.

Ultimately, your success in convincing your teenager not to smoke will depend on the quality of your relationship. If this is the first time the two of you have talked honestly about life and the future, do not expect to be successful. If you have built a strong relationship over the previous sixteen years, this year should go well also.

Now that I've quit smoking, I'm starting to feel a little guilty about my drinking. Do you think I might have a similar sort of problem with drinking?

Nicotine dependence shares characteristics with other chemical dependencies. I have mentioned many of them in this book, particularly in the chapter "Cigarette Smoking Is an Addiction" in Part I (pages 21–50).

In 1991, about 25 percent of adult Americans smoked; about half of them were also dependent on alcohol or some other chemical. Some of them were recovering from their other dependency. (There are about one million recovering alcoholics in Alcoholics Anonymous in the United States.) Thus, there is a good chance that you do have a problem with drinking which you may not have recognized until now.

How will you know? Return to the chapter "Cigarette Smoking Is an Addiction." Read over the characteristics of addictions listed there (page 21), and substitute "alcohol" for the word "chemical." Then pick out any other chapter and substitute the word "alcohol" for the word "nicotine" and the word "drinking" for the word "smoking."

You may have a problem with a chemical other than alcohol. Try substituting the name of the chemical you are concerned about for "nicotine" and the word "using" for "smoking."

If you are constantly thinking about a chemical (alcohol, heroin, cocaine, marijuana, prescription medication, or pain pills); if you cannot predict when or how much of the chemical you will use today; if you have found yourself choosing your chemical over people or activities that you used to like; or if you have continued to use the chemical in spite of significant consequences, you may be dependent on it.

If any of the discussions of dependent behavior still ring true for you, you may have an alcohol or other drug problem. If you are not sure, attend a meeting of Alcoholics Anonymous and introduce yourself as a visitor. If you believe you do have a problem, make an appointment for an evaluation with your doctor, an addictions counselor, a treatment center, or your local chapter of the National Council on Alcoholism and Drug Dependence.

I'm a recovering alcoholic and now I'm a recovering nicotine addict too. My AA meetings are really important to me, but now I can't stand all the smoke at the meetings—you can cut it with a knife. What should I do? I don't want to be around all the smoke, but I really need the AA meetings, and there are very few nonsmoking AA meetings in my area.

More nonsmoking meetings are springing up all the time. Bring the issue up at appropriate meetings from time to time. Ask for a vote during meetings about going smoke-free. Insist on a nonsmoking table in a well-ventilated area.

Many meetings are held in churches, hospitals, and community centers that no longer allow smoking on their premises. These are not always listed as "nonsmoking meetings," because they are nonsmoking by default, not because the members want it that way. Sometimes the building in which a regular (smoking) meeting is held goes smoke-free and the group has to decide to abide by the new rule or move the meeting. You can support staying at the same location and having the meetings be nonsmoking.

When you think about it, all meetings should be nonsmoking. The smoke is an environmental hazard for smokers and nonsmokers alike: all those cigarettes represent a fire hazard, and people pursuing healthy lifestyles should deal with smoking before anything else. You are now aware of how effectively nicotine blunts feelings; Alcoholics Anonymous members value feelings and recognize how they used alcohol and other drugs to suppress them. When they smoke at AA meetings (and they probably smoke more there than elsewhere), their nicotine hides the feelings that come up during the meeting.

You can be an advocate for change. As the number of nonsmokers in AA increases, more meetings will become smoke-free. In another ten or fifteen years, nonsmoking meetings will be as common as smoking meetings. As I write this, your AA schedule notes which meetings are nonsmoking. Eventually, it will note the few remaining smoking meetings, because they will be the exception to the rule.

I've become very depressed since I stopped smoking. I'm thinking of starting again because I feel so awful. I think I was better off when I was smoking.

Nicotine acts like amphetamine and cocaine to relieve depression. Early in his psychiatric career, Freud used cocaine to treat his own depression and recommended it to patients, but he soon learned how dangerous this could be and stopped advocating its use. Freud never did quit smoking, however, and the nicotine in his cigars may have helped relieve his depression.

Today we have many medications to treat depression that are far more effective and much safer than nicotine or cocaine, and even more effective ones are in various stages of development. Researchers are also working to discover which antidepressant medications are effective in alleviating nicotine craving. I strongly recommend you see your doctor or a psychiatrist and describe how you feel; the doctor will either treat you or refer you to someone who will. You do not need to return to smoking because of depression.

Does the research show that my risk of serious illnesses will drop now that I have quit?

In 1990, Surgeon General Dr. Antonia C. Novello released a report on the health benefits of smoking cessation. This six hundred-page volume (which can be purchased from the U.S. Government Printing Office) describes the current research in this area and comes to a number of important conclusions:

1. The risk of having a stroke drops to that of people who never smoked in five to fifteen years after quitting.
2. The risk of developing cancer of the mouth, throat, or esophagus drops by half within five years of quitting.

3. The risk of coronary heart disease drops by half within one year and drops to the rate of people who never smoked in fifteen years.
4. The risk of developing lung cancer drops by half within ten years after quitting.
5. The risk of getting cancer of the pancreas, bladder, larynx, and cervix all drop after quitting.
6. The risk of getting emphysema, ulcers, and arteriosclerosis all drop after quitting.
7. The risk of a woman giving birth to a low-birthweight baby decreases immediately after she quits smoking.

In fact, quitting smoking reduces the risk of getting most of the illnesses associated with smoking. And, as you might have guessed, quitting smoking does not *increase* your risk of getting any known disease.

Where can I learn more about nicotine dependence?

Some two thousand articles about nicotine and nicotine dependence are published in scientific and medical journals each year. Materials for nonscientists and for treatment professionals have been slow to keep pace. Interest in such materials has increased in the last few years, and major publishing houses are now releasing books and pamphlets on nicotine dependence. Check with a medical librarian for professional books and with the publishers of recovery-oriented materials for their most recent publications.

Each year the American Society of Addiction Medicine sponsors the National Conference on Nicotine Dependence. This conference draws speakers and participants from around the country to discuss nicotine, the consequences of its use, and the treatment of nicotine dependence. You can write to the following address for more information about this conference:

American Society of Addiction Medicine
4601 N. Park Drive
Suite 101, Arcade
Chevy Chase, MD 20815
(301) 656-3920

Minnesota Smoke-Free 2000 is a consortium of groups interested in encouraging smoking cessation and the development of smoke-free public buildings and workplaces. You can write to them at this address:

Smoke-Free 2000
420 N. Fifth St., Room 525
Minneapolis, MN 55401
(612) 338-8193

The American Lung Association, the American Cancer Society, the American Heart Association, and several of their chapters regularly sponsor smoking cessation programs and programs on illnesses caused by tobacco. Check with their offices in your community for information.

New conferences and courses on nicotine dependence are being organized all the time. Check with one of the organizations listed or with the Nicotine Dependence Committee of the American Society of Addiction Medicine for current listings.

Now what? I've finished the book.

Now is when the real work begins. Now is when you continue your personal growth in recovery.

You may want to continue in some form of therapy, whether it be group or individual. I strongly suggest you continue with Nicotine Anonymous meetings. You may want to review some of the material in this book on a regular basis, as discussed in the section on relapse prevention planning in chapter 6 of Part III.

Eventually, you may want to be a supporter or sponsor for newcomers in Nicotine Anonymous. You can be a supporter right now, but you should probably wait a year or more before accepting the responsibility of sponsorship. You may even want to help others in a program such as this one, but I suggest you wait until you are at least two years in recovery before you do so. The more responsibility you take on, the more stress you will be under. Be sure your own recovery is stable before you take on these responsibilities.

Can I write to you and tell you how I'm doing?

As you have no doubt noticed, the credit for most of the material in this book goes to the many patients I've worked with over the last twenty years. I look forward to hearing your story as well.

Write to me at the University of Texas Medical School at Houston:

Terry A. Rustin, M.D.
4514 Lyons
Houston, TX 77020

What is the most important thing I need to do to stay quit and not relapse?

Excellent question. You need to . . .

– 13 –

Setting Goals for the Future

This book has taken you from not even considering smoking as a problem to recognizing the problem, making a decision to quit, taking action, finishing your last pack, and making plans to prevent relapse and continue your recovery. Each part asked you to invest time and effort. You have discovered that the more effort you put into this project, the more you benefited.

You began each part by evaluating how you felt and what you believed, and by identifying goals. Having reached the end of this book (but not the end of your journey of recovery), it is now time to identify goals for the future.

Now that you know how to set goals and pursue them, you can continue to do so. Setting goals will help you organize your life and plan your future. Since you have gotten so good at it, why not do it on a regular basis?

✎ *What are your short- and long-term goals for the future? List them in your journal.*

Congratulations and welcome to a smoke-free future.

Bibliography

Brigham, J., J. E. Henningfield, and M. L. Stitzer. 1990. Smoking relapse: A review. *International Journal of the Addictions* 25:1239–55.

A review of factors that predict relapse in people who have quit smoking.

Cook, D. G., P. H. Whincup, M. J. Jarvis, D. P. Strachan, O. Papacosta, and A. Bryant. 1994. Passive exposure to tobacco smoke in children aged five to seven years: Individual, family, and community factors. *British Medical Journal* 308: 384–89.

Children absorb significant amounts of nicotine from parents' smoking.

DiClemente, C. C., J. O. Prochaska, S. K. Fairhurst, W. F. Velicer, M. M. Velasquez, and J. S. Rossi. 1991. The process of smoking cessation: An analysis of precontemplation, contemplation, and preparation stages of change. *Journal of Consulting and Clinical Psychology* 59:295–304.

Smokers move along a continuum of change: precontemplation, contemplation, determination (preparation), action, maintenance . . . and (frequently) relapse. They may remain in relapse, or may re-enter contemplation.

DiFranza, J. R., J. W. Richards, P. M. Paulman, N. Wolf-Gillespie, C. Fletcher, R. D. Jaffe, and D. Murray. 1991. RJR-Nabisco's cartoon camel promotes Camel cigarettes to children. *Journal of the American Medical Association* 266:3149–53.

Camel cigarettes increased market share among children from 0.5 percent to 32.8 percent after the Joe Camel promotion began in 1988.

Ferguson, T. 1988. *The no-nag, no-guilt, do-it-your-own-way guide to quitting smoking.* New York: Ballantine.

Offers a wide variety of helpful suggestions for people who are in early Action stage of quitting.

Fischer, P. M., M. P. Schwartz, J. W. Richards, A. O. Goldstein, and T. H. Rojas. 1991. Brand logo recognition by children aged three to six years: Mickey Mouse and Old Joe the Camel. *Journal of the American Medical Association* 266:3145–48.

Nearly as many six-year-olds recognize Joe Camel as recognize Mickey Mouse (91 percent versus 100 percent).

Glassman, A. H. 1993. Cigarette smoking: Implications for psychiatric illness. *American Journal of Psychiatry* 150:546–53.

Depression and nicotine/tobacco dependence are linked.

Heatherton, T. F., L. T. Kozlowski, R. C. Frecker, and K. O. Fagerström. 1991. The Fagerström Test for Nicotine Dependence: A revision of the Fagerström Tolerance Questionnaire. *British Journal of Addictions* 86:1119–27.
    The Fagerström Test for Nicotine Dependence correlates with cotinine levels.

Henningfield, J. E., and R. M. Keenan. 1993. Nicotine delivery kinetics and abuse liability. *Journal of Consulting and Clinical Psychology* 61:743–50.
    Review of addictive properties of nicotine.

Hurt, R. D., L. C. Dale, P. A. Fredrickson, C. C. Caldwell, G. A. Lee, K. P. Offord, G. G. Lauger, Z. Marusic, L. W. Neese, and T. G. Lundber. 1994. Nicotine patch therapy for smoking cessation combined with physician advice and nurse follow-up. *Journal of the American Medical Association* 271:595–600.
    Nicotine patch doubles quit rate at one year in an intensive smoking cessation program.

Kottke, T. E., R. N. Battista, G. H. DeFriese, and M. L. Brekke. 1988. Attributes of successful smoking cessation interventions in medical practice: A meta-analysis of thirty-nine controlled trials. *Journal of the American Medical Association* 259:2883–89.
    Meta-analysis of 39 studies. 50 percent relapse after one week; 88 percent relapse by one year.

Mulligan, S. C., J. G. Masterson, J. G. Devane, and J. G. Kelly. 1990. Clinical and pharmacokinetic properties of a transdermal nicotine patch. *Clinical Pharmacology and Therapeutics* 47, 331–37.
    Nicotine patch produces steady-state nicotine levels in the range of 10–20 ng/ml.

Orleans, C. T., N. Resch, E. Noll, M. K. Keintz, B. K. Rimer, T. V. Brown, and T. M. Snedden. 1994. Use of transdermal nicotine in a state-level prescription plan for the elderly. *Journal of the American Medical Association* 271:601–07.
    Patch plus ten minutes physician counseling doubles quit rate of the patch without counseling.

Perkins, K. A., L. H. Epstein, B. L. Marks, R. L. Stiller, and R. G. Jacob. 1989. The effect of nicotine on energy expenditure during light physical activity. *New England Journal of Medicine* 320:898–903.
    BMR drops when smokers quit: 5 percent at rest and 12 percent during exercise.

Pomerleau, O. F., C. S. Pomerleau, E. M. Morrell, and J. M. Lownbergh. 1991. Effects of fluoxetine on weight gain and food intake in smokers who reduce nicotine intake. *Psychoneuroendocrinology* 16:433–40.

Giving Prozac prevents weight gain when smokers quit.

Reynolds, P., and T. Shachtman. 1989. *The gilded leaf: Triumph, tragedy and tobacco.* Boston: Little, Brown and Co.

The story of the Reynolds family and the R. J. Reynolds Tobacco Company as told by the grandson of the founder.

Sachs, D. 1986. Cigarette smoking; Health effects and cessation strategies. *Clinics in Geriatric Medicine* 2:337–62.

Extensive review of the benefits of smoking cessation.

Shipley, R. 1990. *QuitSmart: A guide to freedom from cigarettes.* Durham, N.C.: JB Press.

A well-researched cognitive-behavioral approach to quitting smoking.

Transdermal Nicotine Study Group. 1991. Transdermal nicotine for smoking cessation: Six-month results from two multicenter controlled clinical trials. *Journal of the American Medical Association* 266:3133–48.

Nicotine patch doubles quit rate at twenty-four weeks.

U.S. Department of Health and Human Services. 1988. *The health consequences of smoking: Nicotine addiction.* Washington, D.C.: U.S. Department of Health and Human Services, Public Health Service, Office of Smoking and Health, (DHHS Publication 88–8406).

Extensively documented evaluation of the addicting qualities of nicotine.

———. 1990. *The health benefits of smoking cessation: A report of the Surgeon General.* Rockville, Md.: U.S. Department of Health and Human Services, Public Health Service, Office of Smoking and Health.

Important Surgeon General's report that documents the value of smoking cessation.

U.S. Environmental Protection Agency. 1992. *Respiratory health effects of passive smoking: Lung cancer and other disorders.* Washington, D.C.: U.S. Environmental Protection Agency, Office of Health and Environmental Assessment, EPA Publication (EPA/600/6–90/006F).

Extensive documentation of the damage caused by environmental tobacco smoke.

Index

About the Author

Terry A. Rustin, M.D., specializes in addiction medicine. He is assistant professor at the University of Texas Medical School at Houston, and he serves as medical director of the Addiction Treatment Program at Harris County Psychiatric Center. Dr. Rustin is a certified psychodrama therapist and trainer, and is director of Rediscovery: The Psychodrama Institute of the Southwest.

Dr. Rustin has had a special interest in the treatment of nicotine and tobacco dependence since 1979, when he ran his first treatment group—a complete failure. Since then, he has developed a variety of successful strategies for treating nicotine and tobacco dependence and for incorporating its treatment into chemical dependency treatment programs.

Hazelden Foundation, a national nonprofit organization founded in 1949, helps people reclaim their lives from the disease of addiction. Built on decades of knowledge and experience, Hazelden's comprehensive approach to addiction addresses the full range of individual, family, and professional needs, including addiction treatment and continuing care services for youth and adults, publishing, research, higher learning, public education, and advocacy.

A life of recovery is lived "one day at a time." Hazelden publications, both educational and inspirational, support and strengthen lifelong recovery. In 1954, Hazelden published *Twenty-Four Hours a Day,* the first daily meditation book for recovering alcoholics, and Hazelden continues to publish works to inspire and guide individuals in treatment and recovery, and their loved ones. Professionals who work to prevent and treat addiction also turn to Hazelden for evidence-based curricula, informational materials, and videos for use in schools, treatment programs, and correctional programs.

Through published works, Hazelden extends the reach of hope, encouragement, help, and support to individuals, families, and communities affected by addiction and related issues.

For questions about Hazelden publications,
please call **800-328-9000**
or visit us online at **hazelden.org/bookstore.**